Dr Michael M. Gruneberg, designer and writer of the Gruneberg Linkword Language Courses, is widely acknowledged as an international expert on memory improvement. A Senior Lecturer in Psychology at University College, Swansea, he has published a large number of articles in scientific journals, as well as a number of well-known books on the application of memory research. He has also lectured widely in both the UK and the USA and given keynote addresses to several international scientific conferences. In 1988 he provided the original script for, and appeared in, *The Magic of Memory*, a programme in the BBC television QED series which illustrated many memory techniques, including his own Linkword Method, and he recently acted as principal scientific consultant for a major BBC 1 series on memory.

The Linkword Courses have grown out of a large body of published scientific research showing that the imagery method they employ is highly effective in improving the memory for foreign language vocabulary. One study has shown that using this method increases retention from 28% to 88% for a list of 60 Spanish words. Dr Gruneberg has taken this work considerably further, working with linguists and setting out images and testing patterns to create a fully-integrated language-learning system capable of teaching both vocabulary and grammar.

Since it was first published in 1987, the Linkword system has been both highly successful and widely acclaimed and Linkword books are now published throughout the world. Dr Gruneberg works with highly qualified language experts to produce Linkword books which teach you not only **what** to learn, but **how to remember what you have learned**, more quickly and more enjoyably than you ever imagined!

Language Consultants
V.L. Gruneberg. Sheila Jones, M.A., Lecturer in German, University College, Swansea. Graham Coldwell, B.A., Teacher in German, Bishopston School, Swansea.

Also by Dr Michael M. Gruneberg

LINKWORD: FRENCH IN A DAY
LINKWORD LANGUAGE SYSTEM: FRENCH
LINKWORD LANGUAGE SYSTEM: FURTHER FRENCH
LINKWORD: SPANISH IN A DAY
LINKWORD LANGUAGE SYSTEM: SPANISH
LINKWORD LANGUAGE SYSTEM: ITALIAN
LINKWORD LANGUAGE SYSTEM: GREEK
LINKWORD LANGUAGE SYSTEM: PORTUGUESE
(with Dr G.C. Jacobs)

LINKWORD
LANGUAGE SYSTEM

GERMAN

Dr Michael M. Gruneberg

Language Consultants
**V. L. Gruneberg, Sheila Jones
and Graham Coldwell**

CORGI BOOKS

To John Beloff

LINKWORD LANGUAGE SYSTEM – GERMAN
A CORGI BOOK 0 552 13054 0

First publication in Great Britain

PRINTING HISTORY
Corgi edition published 1987
Corgi edition reprinted 1988
Corgi edition reissued 1991
Corgi edition reprinted 1992
Corgi edition reprinted 1993
Corgi edition reprinted 1994

Copyright © Dr Michael Gruneberg 1987

This book is set in 9/10pt Century by Colset Private Limited, Singapore

Corgi Books are published by Transworld Publishers Ltd., 61– 63 Uxbridge Road, Ealing, London W5 5SA, in Australia by Transworld Publishers (Australia) Pty. Ltd., 15– 25 Helles Avenue, Moorebank, NSW 2170, and in New Zealand by Transworld Publishers (N.Z.) Ltd., 3 William Pickering Drive, Albany, Auckland.

Printed and bound in Great Britain by Cox & Wyman Ltd., Reading, Berkshire

Contents

Foreword

Anyone using a book which teaches you a foreign language might well wonder why it has been written by a memory expert and not a linguist or a language teacher. Well, the simple fact is that if you want to *remember* what you are taught, then putting ease of remembering at the centre of the design of the programme is likely to lead to far higher levels of learning than a programme written only with the ideas of a linguist in mind. Of course this programme has been written by a memory expert working with skilled linguists so that the language aspects are correct.

The basic 'memory idea' of the programme which helps so much with remembering what you are taught is the 'method of association' or the **Linkword** method. Learning a foreign language is all about associating what you are familiar with, e.g. the word 'bread' with something you are not familiar with – the word for bread is 'pan' in French or Japanese. Most people repeat the words 'bread' and 'pan' together until they are sure it sticks, but you can link the words together by 'picturing' yourself putting some bread into a pan. This picturing technique is known as the method of association or the **Linkword** method. Of course, as far as learning foreign language vocabulary is concerned, there is a further complication that the foreign word may not sound like any English word. For example the Spanish for cow sounds like Vaka. What you do in this situation is to imagine a *cow* with a *vacuum* cleaner, cleaning a field. The linkword *'vacuum'*, does not have to be identical to the foreign word in order to be able to associate cow with vaka through the use of pictures. It may sound bizarre, but over fifty studies published in respectable scientific journals have found this technique to materially increase the level of foreign vocabulary learning. In one study of Spanish, for example, learning increased from 28% for rote learning to 88% using the picture association technique. The method of association was known to the Greeks as an efficient way of improving memory, and the application of the method of association to learning foreign languages was discussed as long ago as the nineteenth century. It is only recently however, that psychologists have shown how effective the method is when applied to learning foreign language vocabulary, and the present programme is, as far as the author is aware, the first to make use of the method to provide a whole course for foreign language learners, teaching not only an extensive vocabulary but a basic grammar and using sentence examples.

The course consists of hundreds of useful words which, with the grammar provided, can be strung together to form sentences. In eight to twelve hours you should be able to go right through the course and acquire enough useful knowledge to communicate when you go abroad.

The author has published a number of studies* of the courses which show how fast and easy people find it. In one study of travel executives, the group were taught Spanish for *twelve* contact hours. They were then tested by an independent assessor who found they were virtually errorless on the four hundred word vocabulary and grammar they had been taught. The independent assessor estimated they would normally have taken *forty* hours to reach that standard. In a second study, a group of bankers were taught a vocabulary of at least six hundred words and basic grammar in four days. However, it is not just the linguistically able who benefit from the courses. In one study, thirteen-year-old low ability language students were given one session every week using the Spanish Linkword course and another session using conventional teaching methods, for one term. At the end of the term the students were given a test where the mean vocabulary score on Spanish following conventional teaching was 23.75% compared to 69% for the **Linkword** course. One student out of sixteen passed with conventional teaching, fourteen out of sixteen passed with the Spanish Linkword teaching. The studies carried out to date show that the courses are ideal for anyone who wants to learn the basics of a language in a hurry, whether for travel, for business or for school work. For many people such as the holiday-maker who just wants to get by or the business person who has to be in Berlin next Wednesday, then Paris next Friday, their language needs do not involve the mastery of a single language in depth but the rapid acquisition of a basic language to get by with. Because they are designed specifically to enhance speed and ease of language acquisition and to help you remember what you have learned, the **Linkword** courses are uniquely suited to meet such needs as well as the needs of those who might have experienced language learning difficulties earlier in life.

* M.M. Gruneberg and G.J. Jacobs, 'In Defence of Linkword', *Language Learning Journal*, No. 3 (1991), 25–29

INTRODUCTION

TEST YOURSELF WITH LINKWORD

Picture each of these images in your mind's eye for about ten seconds. For example, the French for *tablecloth* is *nappe*. Imagine yourself having a nap on a tablecloth, as vividly as you can, for about ten seconds.

○ The French for TABLECLOTH is NAPPE
Imagine having a *NAP* on a *TABLECLOTH*.

○ The German for GENTLEMEN is HERREN
Imagine a *HERRING* dangling from the door of a *GENTLEMEN'S* toilet.

○ The Italian for FLY is MOSCA.
Imagine *FLIES* invading *MOSCOW*.

○ The Spanish for SUITCASE is MALETA
Imagine *MY LETTER* in your *SUITCASE*.

○ The French for HEDGEHOG is HERISSON.
Imagine your *HAIRY SON* looks like a *HEDGEHOG*.

○ The German for LETTER is BRIEF.
Imagine a *BRIEF LETTER*.

○ The Italian for DRAWER is CASSETTO.
Imagine you keep *CASSETTES* in a *DRAWER*.

○ The Spanish for WAITRESS is CAMARERA.
Imagine a *WAITRESS* with a *CAMERA* slung around her neck!

NOW TURN OVER

○ What is the English for CAMARERA? _____

○ What is the English for CASSETTO? _____

○ What is the English for BRIEF? _____

○ What is the English for HERISSON? _____

○ What is the English for MALETA? _____

○ What is the English for MOSCA? _____

○ What is the English for HERREN? _____

○ What is the English for NAPPE? _____

TURN BACK FOR THE ANSWERS

Do not expect to get them all correct at the first attempt. However, if you feel you got more right than you normally would have — then this course will suit you!

WHO IS LINKWORD FOR?

The short answer is that Linkword is for anyone and everyone who wants to learn the basics of a language in a hurry. It can be used by children or by adults. Even young children who cannot read can be taught German words by a parent reading out the images.

The Linkword Courses have been carefully designed to teach you a basic grammar and words in a simple step-by-step way that anyone can follow. After about 10—12 hours, or even less, you will have a vocabulary of literally hundreds of words and the ability to string these words together to form sentences. The course is ideal, therefore, for the holidaymaker or business person who just wants the basics in a hurry so he or she can be understood, e.g. in the hotel, arriving at the destination, sightseeing, eating out, in emergencies, telling the time and so on.

The course is also an ideal supplement to schoolwork. Many school pupils feel that they remember words for the first time when introduced to the Linkword system, and understand basic grammar for the first time too!

HOW TO USE LINKWORD

1] You will be presented with words like this:
The German for GENTLEMEN is HERREN
Imagine a HERRING dangling from the door of a
GENTLEMEN'S toilet.
What you do is to imagine this picture in your mind's eye as
vividly as possible.

2] After you have read the image you should think about it in your
mind's eye for about 10 seconds before moving on to the next
word. If you do not spend enough time thinking about the image
it will not stick in your memory as well as it should.

3] Sometimes the word in German and in English is the same or
very similar. For example, the German for "taxi" is "taxi". When
this happens you will be asked to associate the word in some way
with the German flag.

Imagine a taxi covered with the German flag. Whenever the
German flag comes to mind, therefore, you will know the word is
the same or similar in both English and German.

4] The examples given in the course may well strike you as silly and
bizarre. They have deliberately been given in this way to show up
points of grammar and to get away from the idea that you should
remember useful phrases "parrot fashion".

5] ACCENTS

In German you sometimes have an accent above vowels, e.g. grün, öl. These accents affect the way the word is pronounced but the approximate pronunciation of these accented words is given in the course, so do not worry about them at this stage. The accent is called an umlaut in German.

6] PRONUNCIATION

The approximate pronunciation of words is given in brackets after the word is presented for the first time.

For example: The German for CURTAIN is GARDINE
(GARDEENEH)
(GARDEENEH) is the way the word is
pronounced.

Do not worry too much about these pronunciations to begin with. The approximate pronunciation given in brackets will allow you to be understood. If you would like to listen to the exact pronunciation, an audio-tape containing all the words on the course is available from Corgi Books.

SOME USEFUL HINTS

1. It is usually best to go through the course as quickly as possible. Many people can get through most of the course in a weekend, especially if they start on Friday evening.

2. Take a break of about 10 minutes between each section, and always *stop* if you feel tired.

3. Don't worry about forgetting a few words, and do not go back to relearn words you have forgotten. Just think of how much you are learning, and try to pick up the forgotten words when it comes to revising.

4. Revise after Section 4, Section 8 and at the end of the course. Then revise the whole course a week later and a month later.

5. Don't worry if you forget some of the words of grammar after a time. Relearning is extremely fast, and going through the book for a few hours just before you go abroad will quickly get you back to where you were.

6. The course will not give you conversational fluency. You can't expect this until you go abroad and live in a country for a period of time. What it will give you very rapidly is the ability to survive in a large number of situations you will meet abroad. Once you have got this framework, you will find it much easier to pick up more words and grammar when you travel.

IMPORTANT NOTE

The first section of the course can be basically regarded as a training section designed to get you into the Linkword method quickly and easily.

After about 45 minutes you will have a vocabulary of about 30 words and be able to translate sentences. Once you have finished Section 1 you will have the confidence to go through the rest of the course just as quickly. Animal words are used in the first section as they are a large group of "easy to image" words. Many animal words of course are useful to have as they are often met abroad, e.g. dog, cat, etc., or they are edible!

Finally, when it comes to translating sentences the answers are given at the foot of the page. You may find it useful to cover up the answers before you tackle the translations.

Section 1   ANIMALS

N.B. The word on the right-hand side of the page (IN BRACKETS) is the way the word is pronounced.

THINK OF EACH IMAGE IN YOUR MIND'S EYE FOR ABOUT TEN SECONDS

○ The German for LOBSTER is HUMMER   (HUMMER)*
   Imagine a lobster with a sense of HUMOUR.

○ The German for SPIDER is SPINNE   (SHPINNEH)
   Imagine a spider SPINNING its web.

○ The German for PIG is SCHWEIN   (SHVINE)*
   Imagine calling your pet pig a rotten SWINE.

○ The German for GOOSE is GANS   (GANS)
   Imagine GANGS of geese going around together.

○ The German for DUCK is ENTE   (ENTEH)
   Imagine a duck ENTERING a room, quacking as it goes.

○ The German for BULL is BULLE   (BULLEH)
   Imagine a BULL on a German flag.

○ The German for COW is KUH   (KOO)
   Imagine a COW standing on the German flag.

○ The German for MIDGE is MÜCKE   (MOOKEH)
   Imagine being MUCKY and attracting midges.

○ The German for MOTH is MOTTE   (MOTTEH)
   Imagine your personal MOTTO is "I like moths."

○ The German for CATERPILLAR is RAUPE   (ROWPEH)
   Imagine a caterpillar with a ROPE attached to its middle.

* The I is pronounced like the I in "wine", the U like the U in "put".

YOU CAN WRITE YOUR ANSWERS IN

○ What is the English for Raupe? _____

○ What is the English for Motte? _____

○ What is the English for Mücke? _____

○ What is the English for Kuh? _____

○ What is the English for Bulle? _____

○ What is the English for Ente? _____

○ What is the English for Gans? _____

○ What is the English for Schwein? _____

○ What is the English for Spinne? _____

○ What is the English for Hummer? _____

TURN BACK FOR THE ANSWERS

ELEMENTARY GRAMMAR

In German each noun (thing) can be masculine, feminine or neuter.

If the noun is MASCULINE, the word for THE is DER.

So,

DER HUMMER is THE LOBSTER

If the noun is FEMININE, the word for THE is DIE (pronounced DEE).

So,

DIE KUH is THE COW

If the noun is NEUTER, the word for THE is DAS.

So,

DAS SCHWEIN is THE PIG

The way you remember genders is to use the same imagery technique that you have just used learning German words.

If the word is MASCULINE, always imagine the word interacting with a boxer — a masculine symbol.

For example,

The gender for LOBSTER is MASCULINE (DER HUMMER)

Imagine a boxer tucking into a meal of lobster.

Every time you see a word with a boxer, you will know the word is masculine.

If the gender is FEMININE, always imagine the word interacting with a beautiful little golden-haired girl.

For example,

The gender for COW is FEMININE

(Die Kuh)

Imagine a little girl milking a cow.

Every time you see a word interacting with a little girl, you will know the word is feminine.

If the gender is NEUTER, always imagine the word interacting with a blazing fire.

For example,

The gender for PIG is NEUTER

(Das Schwein)

Imagine a pig being roasted over an open fire.

Every time you see a word interacting with a fire, you will know the word is neuter.

GENDERS

THINK OF EACH IMAGE IN YOUR MIND'S EYE FOR ABOUT TEN SECONDS

○ The gender of LOBSTER is Masculine: DER HUMMER
  Imagine a boxer tucking into a meal of lobster.

○ The gender of SPIDER is Feminine: DIE SPINNE
  Imagine a little girl frightened by a big spider.

○ The gender of PIG is Neuter: DAS SCHWEIN
  Imagine a pig being roasted over a fire.

○ The gender of GOOSE is Feminine: DIE GANS
  Imagine a little girl carrying a large goose.

○ The gender of DUCK is Feminine: DIE ENTE
  Imagine a little girl chasing a group of ducks.

○ The gender of BULL is Masculine: DER BULLE
  Imagine a boxer punching a fierce bull.

○ The gender of COW is Feminine: DIE KUH
  Imagine a little girl milking a cow.

○ The gender of MIDGE is Feminine: DIE MÜCKE
  Imagine a little girl swiping at midges.

○ The gender of MOTH is Feminine: DIE MOTTE
  Imagine a little girl whacking a moth
  attached to a light.

○ The gender of CATERPILLAR is Feminine: DIE RAUPE
  Imagine a little girl putting caterpillars in a matchbox.

13

YOU CAN WRITE YOUR ANSWERS IN

○ What is the gender and German for caterpillar? _____

○ What is the gender and German for moth? _____

○ What is the gender and German for midge? _____

○ What is the gender and German for cow? _____

○ What is the gender and German for bull? _____

○ What is the gender and German for duck? _____

○ What is the gender and German for goose? _____

○ What is the gender and German for pig? _____

○ What is the gender and German for spider? _____

○ What is the gender and German for lobster? _____

TURN BACK FOR THE ANSWERS

MORE ANIMALS

THINK OF EACH IMAGE IN YOUR MIND'S EYE FOR ABOUT TEN SECONDS

○ The German for DOG is HUND   (HUNT)*
Imagine a HUNT with a whole lot of dogs.

○ The German for CAT is KATZE   (KATSEH)
Imagine a CAT sitting on the German flag.

○ The German for MOUSE is MAUS   (MOWS)
Imagine a MOUSE on a German flag.

○ The German for ELEPHANT is ELEFANT   (ELEFANT)
Imagine an ELEPHANT draped in a German flag.

○ The German for HORSE is PFERD   (PFERT)
Imagine asking how your horse FARED in a horse race.

○ The German for EARTHWORM is WURM   (VURM)
Imagine an earthWORM on a German flag.

○ The German for BEE is BIENE   (BEENEH)
Imagine a bee alighting on a baked BEAN.

○ The German for DEER is HIRSCH   (HIRSH)
Imagine loading a dead deer into a HEARSE.

○ The German for SALMON is LACHS   (LAX)
Imagine thinking "This salmon LACKS
something, perhaps a sauce."

○ The German for TROUT is FORELLE   (FORELLEH)
Imagine having a drunken argument about
whether trout is spelt with FOUR L's.

* The U is pronounced like the U in "put".

15

YOU CAN WRITE YOUR ANSWERS IN

O What is the English for Forelle? _____

O What is the English for Lachs? _____

O What is the English for Hirsch? _____

O What is the English for Biene? _____

O What is the English for Wurm? _____

O What is the English for Pferd? _____

O What is the English for Elefant? _____

O What is the English for Maus? _____

O What is the English for Katze? _____

O What is the English for Hund? _____

TURN BACK FOR THE ANSWERS

GENDERS

THINK OF EACH IMAGE IN YOUR MIND'S EYE FOR ABOUT TEN SECONDS

○ The gender of DOG is Masculine: DER HUND
Imagine a dog fighting a boxer in a ring.

○ The gender of CAT is Feminine: DIE KATZE
Imagine a black and white cat being stroked by a little girl.

○ The gender of MOUSE is Feminine: DIE MAUS
Imagine a little girl being chased by a mouse.

○ The gender of ELEPHANT is Masculine: DER ELEFANT
Imagine a boxer riding an elephant with his boxing gloves on.

○ The gender of HORSE is Neuter: DAS PFERD
Imagine a horse galloping through a fire.

○ The gender of EARTHWORM is Masculine: DER WURM
Imagine a boxer playing with an earthworm.

○ The gender of BEE is Feminine: DIE BIENE
Imagine a bee chasing a little girl.

○ The gender of DEER is Masculine: DER HIRSCH
Imagine a boxer carrying a dead deer over his shoulder.

○ The gender of SALMON is Masculine: DER LACHS
Imagine a boxer tucking into a meal of salmon before a fight.

○ The gender of TROUT is Feminine: DIE FORELLE
Imagine a little girl holding a rainbow trout.

YOU CAN WRITE YOUR ANSWERS IN

○ What is the gender and German for trout? _____

○ What is the gender and German for salmon? _____

○ What is the gender and German for deer? _____

○ What is the gender and German for bee? _____

○ What is the gender and German for worm? _____

○ What is the gender and German for horse? _____

○ What is the gender and German for
elephant? _____

○ What is the gender and German for mouse? _____

○ What is the gender and German for cat? _____

○ What is the gender and German for dog? _____

TURN BACK FOR THE ANSWERS

ELEMENTARY GRAMMAR

Up to this point you have learned the German for a number of nouns (things).

You will have to learn a number of other words, using the same technique you have just used. This time, however, you don't have to learn genders.

USEFUL WORDS

THINK OF EACH IMAGE IN YOUR MIND'S EYE FOR ABOUT TEN SECONDS

○ The German for TIRED is MÜDE   (MOODEH)
  Imagine being MOODY and TIRED.

○ The German for QUICK is SCHNELL   (SHNELL)
  Imagine a terrible SMELL as someone rushes
  by at a very QUICK rate.

○ The German for NOISY is LAUT   (LOWT)
  Imagine a LOUT being NOISY.

○ The German for BIG is GROSS   (GROHSS)
  Imagine someone being BIG and GROSS.

○ The German for EMPTY is LEER   (LAIR)
  Imagine a fox's LAIR completely EMPTY.

○ The German for SMALL is KLEIN   (KLINE)*
  Imagine that Pigmies are inCLINED to be SMALL.

○ The German for HEAVY is SCHWER   (SCHVEHR)
  Imagine SWEARING when you try to lift
  something very HEAVY.

○ The German for LATE is SPÄT   (SHPAIT)
  Imagine hitting your friend with a SPADE
  when he is LATE.

* The I is pronounced like the I in "wine".

YOU CAN WRITE YOUR ANSWERS IN

O What is the English for spät? _____

O What is the English for schwer? _____

O What is the English for klein? _____

O What is the English for leer? _____

O What is the English for gross? _____

O What is the English for laut? _____

O What is the English for schnell? _____

O What is the English for müde? _____

TURN BACK FOR THE ANSWERS

YOU CAN WRITE YOUR ANSWERS IN

○ What is the German for late? _____

○ What is the German for heavy? _____

○ What is the German for small? _____

○ What is the German for empty? _____

○ What is the German for big? _____

○ What is the German for noisy? _____

○ What is the German for quick? _____

○ What is the German for tired? _____

TURN BACK FOR THE ANSWERS

SOME IMPORTANT WORDS

The first word is the word "IS".

In German this is IST.

For example, to say

THE COW *IS* TIRED you say   DIE KUH *IST* MÜDE
THE DOG *IS* NOISY is DER HUND *IST* LAUT

The word WAS is WAR in German
(pronounced VAHR).

For example, to say

THE WORM *WAS* TIRED you say
DER WURM *WAR* MÜDE

Now cover up the answers below and translate the following:

(You can write your answers in)

1. THE SPIDER IS QUICK
2. THE PIG IS NOISY
3. THE BULL IS HEAVY
4. THE DOG IS LATE
5. THE BEE WAS BIG

The answers are:

1. DIE SPINNE IST SCHNELL
2. DAS SCHWEIN IST LAUT
3. DER BULLE IST SCHWER
4. DER HUND IST SPÄT
5. DIE BIENE WAR GROSS

Now cover up the answers below and translate the following

(You can write you answers in)

1. DER HIRSCH WAR SCHNELL
2. DIE MAUS IST LEER
3. DIE FORELLE IST MÜDE
4. DER HUMMER IST SCHWER
5. DIE MOTTE IST KLEIN

The answers are:

1. THE DEER WAS QUICK
2. THE MOUSE IS EMPTY
3. THE TROUT IS TIRED
4. THE LOBSTER IS HEAVY
5. THE MOTH IS SMALL

Now cover up the answers below and translate the following:

(You can write your answers in)

1. THE MIDGE IS NOISY
2. THE HORSE IS BIG
3. THE DUCK IS TIRED
4. THE CAT IS SMALL
5. THE CATERPILLAR IS EMPTY

The answers are:

1. DIE MÜCKE IST LAUT
2. DAS PFERD IST GROSS
3. DIE ENTE IST MÜDE
4. DIE KATZE IST KLEIN
5. DIE RAUPE IST LEER

27

Now cover up the answers below and translate the following

(You can write your answers in)

1. DER HUMMER IST KLEIN
2. DAS SCHWEIN IST GROSS
3. DIE GANS IST MÜDE
4. DER HIRSCH IST LAUT
5. DER LACHS IST SCHNELL

The answers are:

1. THE LOBSTER IS SMALL
2. THE PIG IS BIG
3. THE GOOSE IS TIRED
4. THE DEER IS NOISY
5. THE SALMON IS QUICK

IMPORTANT NOTE

Some of the sentences in this course might strike you as being a bit odd!

However, they have been carefully constructed to make you think much more about what you are translating. This helps the memory process and gets away from the idea of learning useful phrases "parrot fashion".

But, of course, having learned with the help of these seemingly odd sentences you can easily construct your own sentences to suit your particular needs.

Section 2 HOTEL/HOME, FURNITURE, COLOURS

FURNITURE AND FITTINGS

THINK OF EACH IMAGE IN YOUR MIND'S EYE FOR ABOUT TEN SECONDS

○ The German for FURNITURE is MÖBEL   (ME(r)BEL)
  Imagine having very MOBILE furniture.

○ The German for CARPET is TEPPICH   (TEPPICH)*
  Imagine TIPPING rubbish on to your carpet.

○ The German for CURTAIN is GARDINE   (GARDEENEH)
  Imagine your GARDEN surrounded by curtains.

○ The German for BED is BETT   (BETT)
  Imagine your BED covered with a German flag.

○ The German for CUPBOARD is SCHRANK   (SHRANK)
  Imagine your cups and saucers SHRANK
  in size when they crashed into the cupboard.

○ The German for ARMCHAIR is SESSEL   (ZESSEL)
  Imagine CECIL B. De Mille, the film
  director, sitting in an armchair.

○ The German for SHELF is BRETT   (BRETT)
  Imagine loaves of BREAD on a shelf.

○ The German for PIANO is KLAVIER   (KLAVEER)
  Imagine someone very CLEVER playing the piano.

○ The German for CLOCK is UHR   (OOHR)
  Imagine someone asking "Is that YOUR clock?"

○ The German for PICTURE is BILD   (BILT)
  Imagine being BILLED for a picture you have just bought.

* The CH is pronounced like the CH in "loch".

31

YOU CAN WRITE YOUR ANSWERS IN

○ What is the English for Bild? _____

○ What is the English for Uhr? _____

○ What is the English for Klavier? _____

○ What is the English for Brett? _____

○ What is the English for Sessel? _____

○ What is the English for Schrank? _____

○ What is the English for Bett? _____

○ What is the English for Gardine? _____

○ What is the English for Teppich? _____

○ What is the English for Möbel? _____

TURN BACK FOR THE ANSWERS

GENDERS

THINK OF EACH IMAGE IN YOUR MIND'S EYE FOR ABOUT TEN SECONDS

O The gender of FURNITURE is Feminine: DIE MÖBEL
Imagine a little girl sitting on some furniture.
(N.B. FURNITURE is plural and the word for THE
when a word is plural is always DIE.)

O The gender of CARPET is Masculine: DER TEPPICH
Imagine a boxer beating a carpet.

O The gender of CURTAIN is Feminine: DIE GARDINE
Imagine a little girl opening the curtains.

O The gender of BED is neuter: DAS BETT
Imagine someone lighting a fire under your bed.

O The gender of CUPBOARD is Masculine: DER SCHRANK
Imagine locking a boxer in your cupboard.

O The gender of ARMCHAIR is Masculine: DER SESSEL
Imagine a boxer lounging in your armchair.

O The gender of SHELF is Neuter: DAS BRETT
Imagine setting fire to a pile of shelves.

O The gender of PIANO is Neuter: DAS KLAVIER
Imagine a fire on top of a grand piano.

O The gender of CLOCK is Feminine: DIE UHR
Imagine a little girl lifting a big clock.

O The gender of PICTURE is Neuter: DAS BILD
Imagine throwing a picture by an old
master on to the fire in a terrible mistake.

YOU CAN WRITE YOUR ANSWERS IN

○ What is the gender and German for picture?　———————

○ What is the gender and German for clock?　———————

○ What is the gender and German for piano?　———————

○ What is the gender and German for shelf?　———————

○ What is the gender and German for
cupboard?　———————

○ What is the gender and German for bed?　———————

○ What is the gender and German for
curtains?　———————

○ What is the gender and German for carpet?　———————

○ What is the gender and German for
furniture?　———————

TURN BACK FOR THE ANSWERS

SOME COLOURS

THINK OF EACH IMAGE IN YOUR MIND'S EYE FOR ABOUT TEN SECONDS

○ The German for BLACK is SCHWARZ   (SHVARTS)
  Imagine someone with BLACK WARTS on his face.

○ The German for WHITE is WEISS   (VICE)
  Imagine a VICE which you spill WHITE paint over.

○ The German for RED is ROT   (ROHT)
  Imagine a huge ROTating RED blob.

○ The German for GREEN is GRÜN   (GROON)
  Imagine going GREEN after working on the
  GRUNeberg Linkword Language System too long.

○ The German for BROWN is BRAUN   (BROWN)
  Imagine BROWN paint on the German flag.

○ The German for GREY is GRAU   (GROW)*
  Imagine a GREY wolf GROWling.

○ The German for BLUE is BLAU   (BLAU)
  Imagine someone BLOWING until he turns BLUE.

○ The German for ORANGE is ORANGE   (ORANGEH)
  Imagine ORANGES wrapped up in the German flag.

* GROW rhymes with COW

YOU CAN WRITE YOUR ANSWERS IN

○ What is the English for orange?   _____

○ What is the English for blau?   _____

○ What is the English for grau?   _____

○ What is the English for braun?   _____

○ What is the English for grün?   _____

○ What is the English for rot?   _____

○ What is the English for weiss?   _____

○ What is the English for schwarz?   _____

TURN BACK FOR THE ANSWERS

YOU CAN WRITE YOUR ANSWERS IN

○ What is the German for orange? _____

○ What is the German for blue? _____

○ What is the German for grey? _____

○ What is the German for brown? _____

○ What is the German for green? _____

○ What is the German for red? _____

○ What is the German for white? _____

○ What is the German for black? _____

TURN BACK FOR THE ANSWERS

ELEMENTARY GRAMMAR: and; but; or

The German for AND is UND.

(pronounced UNT)

UND and AND sound very similar.

For example,

GRÜN UND SCHWARZ is GREEN AND BLACK

DER HUND UND DAS SCHWEIN is THE DOG AND THE PIG

The German for BUT is ABER.

(pronounced AHBER)

Imagine wanting to live anywhere BUT ABERDEEN.

For example,

MÜDE ABER KLEIN is TIRED BUT SMALL

SCHWER ABER LEER is HEAVY BUT EMPTY

The German for OR is ODER.

(pronounced OHDER)

Imagine an ODOUR must come from you OR me.

For example,

GRAU ODER WEISS is GREY OR WHITE

ORANGE ODER BRAUN is ORANGE OR BROWN

Now cover up the answers below and translate the following:

(You can write your answers in)

1. THE CUPBOARD IS RED OR BLACK
2. THE PIANO WAS WHITE AND GREEN
3. THE SHELF IS BROWN AND GREY
4. THE ELEPHANT WAS TIRED BUT HEAVY
5. THE DOG IS WHITE OR GREEN

The answers are:

1. DER SCHRANK IST ROT ODER SCHWARZ
2. DAS KLAVIER WAR WEISS UND GRÜN
3. DAS BRETT IST BRAUN UND GRAU
4. DER ELEFANT WAR MÜDE ABER SCHWER
5. DER HUND IST WEISS ODER GRÜN

Now cover up the answers below and translate the following:

(You can write your answers in)

1. DER TEPPICH IST KLEIN UND BLAU
2. DER SESSEL IST ROT UND BRAUN
3. DAS BETT IST GROSS ABER LEER
4. DIE UHR IST ROT ODER BLAU
5. DAS BILD IST ORANGE UND GRAU

The answers are:

1. THE CARPET IS SMALL AND BLUE
2. THE ARMCHAIR IS RED AND BROWN
3. THE BED IS BIG BUT EMPTY
4. THE CLOCK IS RED OR BLUE
5. THE PICTURE IS ORANGE AND GREY

ELEMENTARY GRAMMAR

In German you can ask questions simply by putting the verb at the beginning of the sentence.

For example,

IS THE DOG WHITE?   is   IST DER HUND WEISS?

WAS THE PIANO HEAVY? is   WAR DAS KLAVIER SCHWER?

Now cover up the answers below and translate the following:

(You can write your answers in)

1. IS THE BED GREY?
2. WAS THE ARMCHAIR BIG OR SMALL?
3. IS THE SALMON TIRED?
4. IS THE PICTURE GREEN?
5. IS THE DOG BROWN?

The answers are:

1. IST DAS BETT GRAU?
2. WAR DER SESSEL GROSS ODER KLEIN?
3. IST DER LACHS MÜDE?
4. IST DAS BILD GRÜN?
5. IST DER HUND BRAUN?

Now cover up the answers below and translate the following:

(You can write your answers in)

1. IST DIE GANS GRAU ODER BLAU?
2. WAR DIE SPINNE SCHWER UND GROSS?
3. IST DIE MOTTE GRÜN ODER ROT?
4. IST DIE MAUS LAUT UND SCHNELL?
5. WAR DER SCHRANK GROSS ODER KLEIN?

The answers are:

1. IS THE GOOSE GREY OR BLUE?
2. WAS THE SPIDER HEAVY AND BIG?
3. IS THE MOTH GREEN OR RED?
4. IS THE MOUSE NOISY AND QUICK?
5. WAS THE CUPBOARD BIG OR SMALL?

SOME MORE WORDS

THINK OF EACH IMAGE IN YOUR MIND'S EYE FOR ABOUT TEN SECONDS

○ The German for ROOM is ZIMMER   (TSIMMER)
Imagine a room SHIMMERING in the sunshine.

○ The German for BATHROOM is   (BADEHTSIMMER)
BADEZIMMER
Imagine a BAD ROOM is where you
have your bathroom.

○ The German for BEDROOM is   (SHLAHFTSIMMER)
SCHLAFZIMMER
Imagine the room where you always laugh —
the LAUGH ZIMMER is where you sleep.

○ The German for KITCHEN is KÜCHE   (KOOCHEH)
Imagine you always COOK in the kitchen.

○ The German for HOUSE is HAUS   (HOWS)
Imagine your HOUSE covered in the German flag.

○ The German for WINDOW is FENSTER   (FENSTER)
Imagine a girl, and you FENCED HER in with a window.

○ The German for ROOF is DACH   (DACH)
Imagine a DUCK sitting on your roof.

○ The German for WALL is WAND   (VANT)
Imagine a fairy waving a WAND at
your wall, and it falls down.

○ The German for FLOOR is BODEN   (BOHDEN)
Imagine BOATING on your wet floor.

○ The German for LIGHT is LICHT   (LEECHT)*
Imagine you LICKED an electric light.

* The CH is pronounced like the CH in "loch".

YOU CAN WRITE YOUR ANSWERS IN

○ What is the English for Licht? _____

○ What is the English for Boden? _____

○ What is the English for Wand? _____

○ What is the English for Dach? _____

○ What is the English for Fenster? _____

○ What is the English for Haus? _____

○ What is the English for Küche? _____

○ What is the English for Schlafzimmer? _____

○ What is the English for Badezimmer? _____

○ What is the English for Zimmer? _____

TURN BACK FOR THE ANSWERS

GENDERS

THINK OF EACH IMAGE IN YOUR MIND'S EYE FOR ABOUT TEN SECONDS

○ The gender of ROOM is Neuter: **DAS ZIMMER**
Imagine a fire in a room of your house.

○ The gender of BATHROOM is Neuter: **DAS BADEZIMMER**
Imagine a fire in your bathroom.

○ The gender of BEDROOM is Neuter: **DAS SCHLAFZIMMER**
Imagine a fire in your bedroom

○ The gender of KITCHEN is Feminine: **DIE KÜCHE**
Imagine a little girl helping her
mother in the kitchen.

○ The gender of HOUSE is Neuter: **DAS HAUS**
Imagine a house on fire.

○ The gender of WINDOW is Neuter: **DAS FENSTER**
Imagine throwing windows onto a bonfire.

○ The gender of ROOF is Neuter: **DAS DACH**
Imagine your roof on fire and
crashing through the house.

○ The gender of WALL is Feminine: **DIE WAND**
Imagine a little girl being hurt by the falling wall.

○ The gender of FLOOR is Masculine: **DER BODEN**
Imagine a boxer lying flat out on the floor.

○ The gender of LIGHT is Neuter: **DAS LICHT**
Imagine the light from a fire.

YOU CAN WRITE YOUR ANSWERS IN

○ What is the gender and German for light? _____

○ What is the gender and German for floor? _____

○ What is the gender and German for wall? _____

○ What is the gender and German for roof? _____

○ What is the gender and German for
window? _____

○ What is the gender and German for house? _____

○ What is the gender and German for kitchen? _____

○ What is the gender and German for
bedroom? _____

○ What is the gender and German for
bathroom? _____

○ What is the gender and German for room? _____

TURN BACK FOR THE ANSWERS

Now cover up the answers below and translate the following:

(You can write your answers in)

1. IS THE HOUSE WHITE OR GREEN?
2. IS THE ROOF BLACK OR BLUE?
3. THE FLOOR IS EMPTY, BUT THE LIGHT IS BIG
4. IS THE BATHROOM OR THE BEDROOM SMALL?
5. WAS THE KITCHEN SMALL?

The answers are:

1. IST DAS HAUS WEISS ODER GRÜN?
2. IST DAS DACH SCHWARZ ODER BLAU?
3. DER BODEN IST LEER, ABER DAS LICHT IST GROSS
4. IST DAS BADEZIMMER ODER DAS SCHLAFZIMMER KLEIN?
5. WAR DIE KÜCHE KLEIN?

Now cover up the answers below and translate the following:

(You can write your answers in)

1. DAS ZIMMER IST ROT, UND DIE WAND IST KLEIN
2. DAS HAUS IST GROSS, UND DAS DACH IST SCHWER
3. DAS BADEZIMMER IST KLEIN
4. DAS FENSTER IST SCHWARZ
5. DER BODEN IST GROSS, ABER DIE KÜCHE IST KLEIN

The answers are:

1. THE ROOM IS RED, AND THE WALL IS SMALL
2. THE HOUSE IS BIG, AND THE ROOF IS HEAVY
3. THE BATHROOM IS SMALL
4. THE WINDOW IS BLACK
5. THE FLOOR IS BIG, BUT THE KITCHEN IS SMALL

Section 3 CLOTHES/FAMILY WORDS

CLOTHES

THINK OF EACH IMAGE IN YOUR MIND'S EYE FOR ABOUT TEN SECONDS

○ The German for HAT is HUT   (HOOT)
  Imagine you give a HOOT when you see your mother's hat.

○ The German for SHOE is SCHUH   (SHOOH)
  Imagine a SHOE on the German flag.

○ The German for TROUSERS is HOSEN   (HOHSEN)
  Imagine HOSING down a pair of trousers.

○ The German for SKIRT is ROCK   (ROCK)
  Imagine a skirt spread over a large ROCK.

○ The German for SHIRT is HEMD   (HEMT)
  Imagine being HEMMED into a corner by a row of shirts.

○ The German for DRESS is KLEID   (KLITE)*
  Imagine you COLLIDE with a dress.

○ The German for TIE is SCHLIPS   (SHLIPS)
  Imagine someone who SLIPS and gets caught
  up in his tie, so it nearly chokes him.

○ The German for SOCKS is SOCKEN   (ZOCKEN)
  Imagine your dirty SOCKS lying on the German flag.

○ The German for COAT is MANTEL   (MANTEL)
  Imagine someone trying to disMANTLE you coat.

○ The German for BLOUSE is BLUSE   (BLOOSEH)
  Imagine someone with a BLUE blouse.

* The I sounds like the I in "wine".

YOU CAN WRITE YOUR ANSWERS IN

○ What is the English for Bluse? _____

○ What is the English for Mantel? _____

○ What is the English for Socken? _____

○ What is the English for Schlips? _____

○ What is the English for Kleid? _____

○ What is the English for Hemd? _____

○ What is the English for Rock? _____

○ What is the English for Hosen? _____

○ What is the English for Schuh? _____

○ What is the English for Hut? _____

TURN BACK FOR THE ANSWERS

GENDERS

THINK OF EACH IMAGE IN YOUR MIND'S EYE FOR ABOUT TEN SECONDS

○ The gender of HAT is Masculine: DER HUT
  Imagine a boxer boxing with a hat on.

○ The gender of SHOE is Masculine: DER SCHUH
  Imagine a boxer throwing a shoe at his opponent.

○ The gender of TROUSERS is Feminine: DIE HOSEN
  Imagine a little girl trying trousers on.
  (In fact, HOSEN is the plural of the
  Feminine noun DIE HOSE.)

○ The gender of SKIRT is Masculine: DER ROCK
  Imagine a boxer dressed in a skirt.

○ The gender of SHIRT is Neuter: DAS HEMD
  Imagine burning your shirt on the fire.

○ The gender of DRESS is Neuter: DAS KLEID
  Imagine someone throwing a dress on a fire.

○ The gender of TIE is Masculine: DER SCHLIPS
  Imagine a boxer putting a tie on before
  going out to fight.

○ The gender of SOCKS is Feminine: DIE SOCKEN
  Imagine a little girl putting her socks on.
  (In fact, SOCKEN is the plural of the
  feminine noun DIE SOCKE.)

○ The gender of COAT is Masculine: DER MANTEL
  Imagine a boxer draped in a heavy coat.

○ The gender of BLOUSE is Feminine: DIE BLUSE
  Imagine a little girl with a beautiful new party blouse.

YOU CAN WRITE YOUR ANSWERS IN

○ What is the gender and German for blouse? _____

○ What is the gender and German for coat? _____

○ What is the gender and German for socks? _____

○ What is the gender and German for tie? _____

○ What is the gender and German for dress? _____

○ What is the gender and German for shirt? _____

○ What is the gender and German for skirt? _____

○ What is the gender and German for
trousers? _____

○ What is the gender and German for shoe? _____

○ What is the gender and German for hat? _____

TURN BACK FOR THE ANSWERS

FAMILY WORDS

THINK OF EACH IMAGE IN YOUR MIND'S EYE FOR ABOUT TEN SECONDS

○ The German for FATHER is VATER   (FAHTTER)
Imagine your father getting FATTER and fatter.

○ The German for MOTHER is MUTTER   (MUTTER)*
Imagine your mother MUTTERING away to herself.

○ The German for BROTHER is BRUDER   (BROODER)
Imagine you have a brother who BROODS a great deal.

○ The German for SISTER is SCHWESTER   (SHVESTER)
Imagine a SWEATER on you sister.

○ The German for HUSBAND is MANN   (MANN)
Imagine the first MAN you see is your husband.

○ The German for WIFE is FRAU   (FROW)
Imagine a FROWN on your wife.

○ The German for SON is SOHN   (ZOHN)
Imagine your son has SOWN his wild oats.

○ The German for DAUGHTER is TOCHTER   (TOCHTER)
Imagine saying "I TAUGHT HER, your daughter."

○ The German for BOY is JUNGE   (YUNGEH)*
Imagine a group of YOUNG boys.

○ The German for GIRL is MÄDCHEN   (MAIDCHEN)
Imagine a group of little MAIDENS, girls of course.

* The U is pronounced as the U in "put".

YOU CAN WRITE YOUR ANSWERS IN

○ What is the English for Mädchen?   _____

○ What is the English for Junge?   _____

○ What is the English for Tochter?   _____

○ What is the English for Sohn?   _____

○ What is the English for Frau?   _____

○ What is the English for Mann?   _____

○ What is the English for Schwester?   _____

○ What is the English for Bruder?   _____

○ What is the English for Mutter?   _____

○ What is the English for Vater?   _____

TURN BACK FOR THE ANSWERS

GENDERS

The gender of:

GIRL is NEUTER
[DAS MÄDCHEN]

Imagine a little girl playing with fire.

All other family words have genders which agree with the sex, so they will be given here:

THE FATHER	is	DER VATER
THE MOTHER	is	DIE MUTTER
THE BROTHER	is	DER BRUDER
THE SISTER	is	DIE SCHWESTER
THE HUSBAND	is	DER MANN
THE WIFE	is	DIE FRAU
THE SON	is	DER SOHN
THE DAUGHTER	is	DIE TOCHTER
THE BOY	is	DER JUNGE
THE GIRL	is	DAS MÄDCHEN

YOU CAN WRITE YOUR ANSWERS IN

○ What is the gender and German for girl?   _____

○ What is the gender and German for boy?   _____

○ What is the gender and German for
daughter?   _____

○ What is the gender and German for son?   _____

○ What is the gender and German for wife?   _____

○ What is the gender and German for
husband?   _____

○ What is the gender and German for sister?   _____

○ What is the gender and German for brother?   _____

○ What is the gender and German for mother?   _____

○ What is the gender and German for father?   _____

TURN BACK FOR THE ANSWERS

SOME MORE USEFUL WORDS

THINK OF EACH IMAGE IN YOUR MIND'S EYE FOR ABOUT TEN SECONDS

○ The German for ONLY is NUR   (NOOR)
  Imagine thinking "If ONLY I KNEW HER."

○ The German for VERY is SEHR   (ZAIR)
  Imagine feeling VERY keen to SEE HER.

○ The German for YES is JA   (YA)
  Imagine your mother saying "YES, take the JAR."

○ The German for NO is NEIN   (NINE)
  Imagine being told NO! NINE times.

○ The German for ALSO is AUCH   (OWCH)
  Imagine you ALSO say OW!

○ The German for NOT is NICHT   (NEECHT)
  Imagine thinking "I hope this is NOT NICKED."

○ The German for QUITE is GANZ   (GANTS)
  Imagine GANGS make you QUITE frightened.

○ The German for THIS is DIES   (DEES)
  Imagine thinking THIS is a TEASE.

○ The German for THAT is DAS   (DAS)
  Imagine thinking "THAT DUST is thick."

○ The German for THERE is DA   (DAH)
  Imagine a child saying to his father "THERE, there DA DA."

YOU CAN WRITE YOUR ANSWERS IN

○ What is the English for da?   _____

○ What is the English for das?   _____

○ What is the English for dies?   _____

○ What is the English for ganz?   _____

○ What is the English for auch?   _____

○ What is the English for nicht?   _____

○ What is the English for nein?   _____

○ What is the English for ja?   _____

○ What is the English for sehr?   _____

○ What is the English for nur?   _____

TURN BACK FOR THE ANSWERS

YOU CAN WRITE YOUR ANSWERS IN

O **What is the German for there?** _____

O **What is the German for that?** _____

O **What is the German for this?** _____

O **What is the German for quite?** _____

O **What is the German for also?** _____

O **What is the German for not?** _____

O **What is the German for no?** _____

O **What is the German for yes?** _____

O **What is the German for very?** _____

O **What is the German for only?** _____

TURN BACK FOR THE ANSWERS

Now cover up the answers below and translate the following:

(You can write your answers in)

1. DAS KLEID IST NUR GRÜN, UND DER SCHLIPS IST NUR BLAU

2. IST DER MANTEL SEHR GROSS UND WEISS?

3. NEIN, DER VATER IST NICHT KLEIN, UND DIE MUTTER IST NICHT GROSS, ABER DER SOHN IST SEHR GROSS

4. WAR DER MANN LAUT, UND WAR DAS MÄDCHEN SPÄT?

5. DIE FRAU IST SCHNELL, ABER DIE TOCHTER IST MÜDE

The answers are:

1. THE DRESS IS ONLY GREEN, AND THE TIE IS ONLY BLUE

2. IS THE COAT VERY BIG AND WHITE?

3. NO, THE FATHER IS NOT SMALL, AND THE MOTHER IS NOT BIG, BUT THE SON IS VERY BIG

4. WAS THE HUSBAND NOISY, AND WAS THE GIRL LATE?

5. THE WIFE IS QUICK, BUT THE DAUGHTER IS TIRED

ELEMENTARY GRAMMAR

Personal pronouns

The German for I is ICH.
(pronounced EECH)

The German for I AM is ICH BIN.

Imagine thinking "I AM A BIN."

So,

ICH BIN MÜDE is I AM TIRED
ICH BIN WEISS is I AM WHITE

Now cover up the answers below and translate the following:

(You can write your answers in)

1. I AM GREEN
2. I AM VERY TIRED
3. AM I BIG OR EMPTY?
4. NO, I AM NOT VERY BLACK
5. I AM NOT HEAVY

The answers are:

1. ICH BIN GRÜN
2. ICH BIN SEHR MÜDE
3. BIN ICH GROSS ODER LEER?
4. NEIN, ICH BIN NICHT SEHR SCHWARZ
5. ICH BIN NICHT SCHWER

Now cover up the answers below and translate the following:

(You can write your answers in)

1. ICH BIN ROT UND GROSS
2. ICH BIN NICHT KLEIN
3. ICH BIN AUCH SPÄT
4. JA, ICH BIN SEHR WEISS
5. NEIN, ICH BIN NICHT LEER ODER LAUT

The answers are:

1. I AM RED AND BIG
2. I AM NOT SMALL
3. I AM ALSO LATE
4. YES, I AM VERY WHITE
5. NO, I AM NOT EMPTY OR NOISY

ELEMENTARY GRAMMAR

"You are"

The German for YOU is DU.

Imagine the phrase "How do YOU DO?"

The German for ARE is BIST.

Imagine telling someone that you think you ARE the BEST.

So,

to say YOU ARE LATE   you say DU BIST SPÄT

to say YOU ARE HEAVY you say DU BIST SCHWER

PLEASE NOTE

The German DU for YOU is used only when you know someone quite well; for example, when you say to your friend "you are black".

When you have just met someone for the first time YOU is SIE in German (pronounced ZEE).

To say YOU ARE, in this case, you say SIE SIND (pronounced ZINT).

Imagine you ARE SINNED against.

So,

The German for YOU ARE is DU BIST when you know someone well, or,

SIE SIND when you do not know someone well.

You also use the word SIND for ARE in sentences such as:

THE CAT AND THE DOG ARE BLACK

In German this sentence is:

DER HUND UND DIE KATZE SIND SCHWARZ

The word SIND is the normal word for ARE.

Now cover up the answers below and translate the following:

(You can write your answers in)

1. YOU ARE NOT TIRED (said to a friend)
2. THE SHIRT AND THE SKIRT ARE VERY BLUE
3. NO, THE SHOE AND THE HAT ARE NOT BIG
4. YOU ARE VERY NOISY, AND I AM VERY HEAVY (not to a friend)
5. YES, YOU ARE ALSO QUITE LATE (to a friend)

The answers are:

1. DU BIST NICHT MÜDE
2. DAS HEMD UND DER ROCK SIND SEHR BLAU
3. NEIN, DER SCHUH UND DER HUT SIND NICHT GROSS
4. SIE SIND SEHR LAUT, UND ICH BIN SEHR SCHWER
5. JA, DU BIST AUCH GANZ SPÄT

Now cover up the answers below and translate the following:

(You can write your answers in)

1. DU BIST NUR KLEIN
2. SIE SIND SEHR GROSS UND SCHWER
3. DU BIST AUCH SPÄT
4. SIE SIND GANZ SCHNELL ABER MÜDE
5. DU BIST GRAU, BLAU UND ORANGE
6. DER VATER UND DIE MUTTER SIND SEHR SCHWARZ

The answers are:

1. YOU ARE ONLY SMALL
2. YOU ARE VERY BIG AND HEAVY (not to a friend)
3. YOU ARE ALSO LATE
4. YOU ARE QUITE QUICK BUT TIRED
5. YOU ARE GREY, BLUE AND ORANGE
6. THE FATHER AND THE MOTHER ARE VERY BLACK

ELEMENTARY GRAMMAR

"He, she and it"

In the last grammar section you were taught that I AM is ICH BIN, and that DU BIST and SIE SIND are YOU ARE.

Now we will look at the words HE, SHE and IT.

The German for HE is ER.

(pronounced AIR)

Imagine thinking "HE always ERRS when he speaks."

For example,

HE IS LATE   is ER IST SPÄT
IST ER SCHWARZ? is IS HE BLACK?

The German for SHE is SIE.
(pronounced ZEE)

So,

SIE IST   is SHE IS
SIE IST MÜDE is SHE IS TIRED

The German for IT is ES.
(pronounced ES)

Imagine IT is an "S" bend.

So,

IT IS   is ES IST
ES IST SPÄT   is IT IS LATE
IST ES SPÄT? is IS IT LATE?

In summary:

ICH BIN SCHWARZ   is I AM BLACK
DU BIST SCHWARZ   is YOU ARE BLACK (to a friend)
SIE SIND SCHWARZ   is YOU ARE BLACK (not to a friend)
ER IST SCHWARZ   is HE IS BLACK
SIE IST SCHWARZ   is SHE IS BLACK
SIE SIND   is YOU ARE
SIE IST   is SHE IS

Finally, the German for WE is WIR (pronounced VEER)

Imagine WE are VEERing all over the road.

So,

WE ARE BLACK is WIR SIND SCHWARZ

Now cover up the answers below and translate the following:

(You can write your answers in)

1. SHE IS TIRED AND EMPTY
2. HE IS ONLY GREEN
3. YOU ARE VERY HEAVY (to a friend)
4. IT IS WHITE AND BROWN
5. YOU ARE NOT LATE (not to a friend)

The answers are:

1. SIE IST MÜDE UND LEER
2. ER IST NUR GRÜN
3. DU BIST SEHR SCHWER
4. ES IST WEISS UND BRAUN
5. SIE SIND NICHT SPÄT

Now cover up the answers below and translate the following:

(You can write your answers in)

1. SIE IST NUR KLEIN
2. ER IST SEHR GROSS UND SEHR SCHWER
3. ES IST GRÜN, WEISS UND BLAU ABER NICHT BRAUN
4. DAS BILD UND DIE GARDINE SIND AUCH ROT
5. DAS BETT UND DAS BRETT SIND SCHWER, ABER ER IST GANZ KLEIN

The answers are:

1. SHE IS ONLY SMALL
2. HE IS VERY BIG AND VERY HEAVY
3. IT IS GREEN, WHITE AND BLUE BUT NOT BROWN
4. THE PICTURE AND THE CURTAIN ARE ALSO RED
5. THE BED AND THE SHELF ARE HEAVY, BUT HE IS QUITE SMALL

Section 4   SOME USEFUL WORDS, TIME WORDS

THINK OF EACH IMAGE IN YOUR MIND'S EYE FOR ABOUT TEN SECONDS

○ The German for LAWN is RASEN   (RAHSEN)
   Imagine RAISINS spread all over your lawn.

○ The German for FLOWER is BLUME   (BLOOMEH)
   Imagine watching a flower BLOOMING.

○ The German for WASP is WESPE   (VESPEH)
   Imagine a wasp which WHISPERS in your ear.

○ The German for TREE is BAUM   (BOWM)
   Imagine a tree BOWING in the wind.

YOU CAN WRITE YOUR ANSWERS IN

○ What is the English for Baum?   _____

○ What is the English for Wespe?   _____

○ What is the English for Blume?   _____

○ What is the English for Rasen?   _____

TURN BACK FOR THE ANSWERS

GENDERS

THINK OF EACH IMAGE IN YOUR MIND'S EYE FOR ABOUT TEN SECONDS

○ The gender of LAWN is Masculine: DER RASEN
  Imagine a boxer standing on the lawn.

○ The gender of FLOWER is Feminine: DIE BLUME
  Imagine a little girl picking flowers.

○ The gender of WASP is Feminine: DIE WESPE
  Imagine a wasp stinging a little girl.

○ The gender of TREE is Masculine: DER BAUM
  Imagine a boxer stuck up a tree.

YOU CAN WRITE YOUR ANSWERS IN

○ What is the gender and German for tree? _____

○ What is the gender and German for wasp? _____

○ What is the gender and German for flower? _____

○ What is the gender and German for lawn? _____

TURN BACK FOR THE ANSWERS

TIME

THINK OF EACH IMAGE IN YOUR MIND'S EYE FOR ABOUT TEN SECONDS

○ The German for TIME IS ZEIT   (TSITE)*
Imagine being told not to lose SIGHT of the time.

○ The German for SECOND is SEKUNDE   (SEKUNDEH)
Imagine waving the German flag every time
the clock moves one SECOND.

○ The German for MINUTE is MINUTE   (MINOOTEH)
Imagine shouting, "Wait a MINUTE, I'll just
get the German flag."

○ The German for HOUR is STUNDE   (SHTUNDEH)
Imagine feeling STUNNED when you are told
there will be no bus for another hour.

○ The German for DAY is TAG   (TAHG)
Imagine someone putting a TAG on the wall
of his prison to count every day that goes by.

○ The German for WEEK is WOCHE   (VOCHEH)
Imagine a girl being so very tired that you
only WOKE HER after she has slept for a week.

○ The German for MONTH is MONAT   (MOHNAT)
Imagine a girl who you MOAN AT once a month.

○ The German for YEAR is JAHR   (YAHR)
Imagine you clearing your YARD out once a year.

○ The German for EVENING is ABEND   (AHBENT)
Imagine driving round A BEND as evening draws in.

○ The German for MORNING is MORGEN   (MORGEN)
Imagine meeting a Welshman called
MORGAN this morning.

* The I is pronounced like the I in "wine".

YOU CAN WRITE YOUR ANSWERS IN

○ What is the English for Morgen? _____

○ What is the English for Abend? _____

○ What is the English for Jahr? _____

○ What is the English for Monat? _____

○ What is the English for Woche? _____

○ What is the English for Tag? _____

○ What is the English for Stunde? _____

○ What is the English for Minute? _____

○ What is the English for Sekunde? _____

○ What is the English for Zeit? _____

TURN BACK FOR THE ANSWERS

GENDERS

THINK OF EACH IMAGE IN YOUR MIND'S EYE FOR ABOUT TEN SECONDS

○ The gender of TIME is Feminine: DIE ZEIT
  Imagine a little girl taking a long time to go to bed.

○ The gender of SECOND is Feminine: DIE SEKUNDE
  Imagine a little girl counting the seconds ticking from a watch.

○ The gender of MINUTE is Feminine: DIE MINUTE
  Imagine a little girl being told to go to bed in a minute.

○ The gender of HOUR is Feminine: DIE STUNDE
  Imagine a little girl standing at a bus stop for an hour.

○ The gender of DAY is Masculine: DER TAG
  Imagine a boxer who eats a huge steak every day.

○ The gender of WEEK is Feminine: DIE WOCHE
  Imagine a little girl sleeping for a week.

○ The gender for MONTH is Masculine: DER MONAT
  Imagine a boxer punch drunk because he has a fight once a month.

○ The gender for YEAR is Neuter: DAS JAHR
  Imagine lighting a bonfire once a year to celebrate a holiday.

○ The gender for EVENING is Masculine: DER ABEND
  Imagine a boxer late one evening.

○ The gender of MORNING is Masculine: DER MORGEN
  Imagine meeting a boxer called Morgan one morning.

YOU CAN WRITE YOUR ANSWERS IN

○ What is the gender and German for
morning?   _____

○ What is the gender and German for
evening?   _____

○ What is the gender and German for year?   _____

○ What is the gender and German for month? _____

○ What is the gender and German for week?   _____

○ What is the gender and German for day?   _____

○ What is the gender and German for hour?   _____

○ What is the gender and German for minute? _____

○ What is the gender and German for second? _____

○ What is the gender and German for time?   _____

TURN BACK FOR THE ANSWERS

ADJECTIVES AND OTHER WORDS

For this section you do not have to learn any genders.

THINK OF EACH IMAGE IN YOUR MIND'S EYE FOR ABOUT TEN SECONDS

○ The German for TODAY is HEUTE   (HOITEH)
  Imagine feeling HAUGHTY TODAY.

○ The German for SOON is BALD   (BALT)
  Imagine looking in a mirror and thinking "I shall SOON be BALD."

○ The German for MORE is MEHR   (MAIR)
  Imagine feeding a MARE MORE food.

○ The German for MUCH is VIEL   (FEEL)
  Imagine thinking "That does not FEEL MUCH."

○ The German for GOOD is GUT   (GOOT)
  Imagine feeling GOOD after waving the German flag.

○ The German for BAD is SCHLECHT   (SHLECHT)
  Imagine being hit by a BAD SLEDGE.

○ The German for ALWAYS is IMMER   (IMMER)
  Imagine thinking "It's ALWAYS HIM-HER — never me."

○ The German for STILL is NOCH   (NOCH)
  Imagine you can STILL hear a KNOCK at the door.

○ The German for HERE is HIER   (HEER)
  Imagine thinking "HERE! HERE!"

YOU CAN WRITE YOUR ANSWERS IN

○ What is the English for hier? _____

○ What is the English for noch? _____

○ What is the English for immer? _____

○ What is the English for schlecht? _____

○ What is the English for gut? _____

○ What is the English for viel? _____

○ What is the English for mehr? _____

○ What is the English for bald? _____

○ What is the English for heute? _____

TURN BACK FOR THE ANSWERS

YOU CAN WRITE YOUR ANSWERS IN

○ What is the German for here? _____

○ What is the German for still? _____

○ What is the German for always? _____

○ What is the German for bad? _____

○ What is the German for good? _____

○ What is the German for much? _____

○ What is the German for more? _____

○ What is the German for soon? _____

○ What is the German for today? _____

TURN BACK FOR THE ANSWERS

Now cover up the answers below and translate the following:

(You can write your answers in)

1. THE TREE IS STILL HEAVY
2. THE LAWN AND THE FLOWER ARE ALWAYS HERE
3. THE HOUR AND THE DAY ARE SOON HERE
4. THE MONTH WAS BLACK
5. THE CARPET AND THE BLOUSE ARE THERE

The answers are:

1. DER BAUM IST NOCH SCHWER
2. DER RASEN UND DIE BLUME SIND IMMER HIER
3. DIE STUNDE UND DER TAG SIND BALD HIER
4. DER MONAT WAR SCHWARZ
5. DER TEPPICH UND DIE BLUSE SIND DA

Now cover up the answers below and translate the following:

(You can write your answers in)

1. DER BODEN IST NICHT MEHR HIER
2. DIE WOCHE WAR NICHT GUT, UND DAS JAHR WAR SEHR SCHLECHT
3. DIE GARDINE ODER DER HUT IST HEUTE ROT
4. DIE WESPE IST IMMER SCHNELL
5. DER MORGEN UND DER ABEND SIND BALD HIER

The answers are:

1. THE FLOOR IS NOT ANYMORE HERE
2. THE WEEK WAS NOT GOOD, AND THE YEAR WAS VERY BAD
3. THE CURTAIN OR THE HAT IS RED TODAY
   (Note the word order for HEUTE)
4. THE WASP IS ALWAYS QUICK
5. THE MORNING AND THE EVENING ARE SOON HERE

ELEMENTARY GRAMMAR

Word order

The important thing about word order is that the verb is always the second idea in a sentence.

This means that sometimes you have to change the normal word order.

For example,

THAT I AM   is DAS *BIN* ICH

TOMORROW I AM THE DOG is MORGEN *BIN* ICH DER
                                                      HUND

BIN is the second word in these sentences.

Another example is:

TODAY HE IS TIRED is HEUTE *IST* ER MÜDE

REMEMBER, the verb is the SECOND IDEA in the sentence. In many cases, however, sentences will be spoken in the same order as in English.

Do not worry if you get the word order wrong to begin with, you will still be understood.

PLEASE NOTE TOO, that the words YES and NO at the beginning of the sentence count as separate sentences. They are not the first idea.

So,

YES, IT IS THE DOG   is JA, ES IST DER HUND

NO, IT IS NOT THE FLOWER is NEIN, ES IST NICHT DIE
                                                      BLUME

ALSO NOTE that the word MORGEN can mean
MORNING or TOMORROW.

Now cover up the answers below and translate the following:

(You can write your answers in)

1. NO, IT IS NOT THE DAY
2. TODAY IT IS HERE
3. THAT IS MORE GREEN
4. YES, IT IS NOT GOOD
5. THE CUPBOARD IS NOT BAD

The answers are:

1. NEIN, ES IST NICHT DER TAG
2. HEUTE IST ES HIER
3. DAS IST MEHR GRÜN
4. JA, ES IST NICHT GUT
5. DER SCHRANK IST NICHT SCHLECHT

Now cover up the answers below and translate the following:

(You can write your answers in)

1. IST DAS SEHR GUT, UND IST DIES SEHR SCHLECHT?
2. DER JUNGE IST HEUTE SEHR GUT
3. DER BRUDER UND DIE SCHWESTER SIND BALD MÜDE
4. WAR DIE BLUSE NICHT BLAU ODER GRÜN?
5. DU BIST NOCH SEHR GUT

The answers are:

1. IS THAT VERY GOOD, AND IS THIS VERY BAD?
2. THE BOY IS VERY GOOD TODAY
3. THE BROTHER AND THE SISTER ARE SOON TIRED
4. WAS THE BLOUSE NOT BLUE OR GREEN?
5. YOU ARE STILL VERY GOOD

Section 5 IN THE RESTAURANT, NUMBERS, TELLING THE TIME

RESTAURANT AND FOOD

THINK OF EACH IMAGE IN YOUR MIND'S EYE FOR ABOUT TEN SECONDS

○ The German for RESTAURANT is   (RESTORANT)
RESTAURANT
Imagine a RESTAURANT with the
German flag draped over the front.

○ The German for TABLE IS TISCH   (TISH)
Imagine TISSUES spread all over the table.

○ The German for WAITER is OBER   (OHBER)
Imagine a waiter carrying a plate of AUBERgines.

○ The German for CUP is TASSE   (TASSEH)
Imagine a TASSLE hanging from the handle of a cup.

○ The German for SAUCER is   (UNTERTASSEH)*
UNTERTASSE
Imagine a tassle under a cup, and a saucer
UNDER the TASSLE.

○ The German for BOTTLE is FLASCHE   (FLASHEH).
Imagine a bottle FLASHING past your head.

○ The German for PLATE is TELLER   (TELLER)
Imagine bank TELLERS at your bank all
have plates in front of them.

○ The German for KNIFE is MESSER   (MESSER)
Imagine someone making a MESS
cutting the meat with a knife.

○ The German for FORK is GABEL   (GAHBEL)
Imagine a group of women GABBLING
away to each other, and poking each other with forks.

○ The German for SPOON is LÖFFEL   (LE(r)FFEL)
Imagine watching whilst the wall of a
gentlemen's LOO FELL and the men
inside are holding spoons.

The U is pronounced like the U in "put".

YOU CAN WRITE YOUR ANSWERS IN

O **What is the English for Löffel?** _____

O **What is the English for Gabel?** _____

O **What is the English for Messer?** _____

O **What is the English for Teller?** _____

O **What is the English for Flasche?** _____

O **What is the English for Untertasse?** _____

O **What is the English for Tasse?** _____

O **What is the English for Ober?** _____

O **What is the English for Tisch?** _____

O **What is the English for Restaurant?** _____

TURN BACK FOR THE ANSWERS

GENDERS

THINK OF EACH IMAGE IN YOUR MIND'S EYE FOR ABOUT TEN SECONDS

○ The gender of RESTAURANT is Neuter: DAS RESTAURANT
Imagine a fire gutting a restaurant.

○ The gender of TABLE is Masculine: DER TISCH
Imagine a boxer banging his fist on the table.

○ The gender of WAITER is Masculine: DER OBER
Imagine a waiter with boxing gloves on.

○ The gender of CUP is Feminine: DIE TASSE
Imagine a little girl throwing a cup at you.

○ The gender of SAUCER is Feminine: DIE UNTERTASSE
Imagine a little girl throwing the
saucer at you after she has thrown the cup.

○ The gender of BOTTLE is Feminine: DIE FLASCHE
Imagine a little girl drinking out of a milk bottle.

○ The gender of PLATE is Masculine: DER TELLER
Imagine a boxer smashing a plate over his opponent.

○ The gender of KNIFE is Neuter: DAS MESSER
Imagine someone poking the fire with a knife.

○ The gender of FORK is Feminine: DIE GABEL
Imagine a little girl poking you with a fork.

○ The gender of SPOON is Masculine: DER LÖFFEL
Imagine a boxer with boxing gloves
on trying to sup his soup with a spoon.

YOU CAN WRITE YOUR ANSWERS IN

○ What is the gender and German for spoon?   _____

○ What is the gender and German for fork?   _____

○ What is the gender and German for knife?   _____

○ What is the gender and German for plate?   _____

○ What is the gender and German for bottle?   _____

○ What is the gender and German for saucer?   _____

○ What is the gender and German for cup?   _____

○ What is the gender and German for waiter?   _____

○ What is the gender and German for table?   _____

○ What is the gender and German for restaurant?   _____

TURN BACK FOR THE ANSWERS

QUESTION WORDS

THINK OF EACH IMAGE IN YOUR MIND'S EYE FOR ABOUT TEN SECONDS

○ The German for WHY is WARUM   (VARUM)
Imagine asking, "Why is it so WARM?"

○ The German for WHO is WER   (VAIR)
Imagine asking, "WHO would WEAR that?"

○ The German for HOW is WIE   (VEE)
Imagine asking HOW you make the V in Vienna.

○ The German for WHAT is WAS   (VAS)
Imagine asking WHAT the FUSS is about.

○ The German for WHERE is WO   (VOH)
Imagine asking WHERE the FOE is.

YOU CAN WRITE YOUR ANSWERS IN

○ What is the English for wo?   _____

○ What is the English for was?   _____

○ What is the English for wie?   _____

○ What is the English for wer?   _____

○ What is the English for warum?   _____

TURN BACK FOR THE ANSWERS

YOU CAN WRITE YOUR ANSWERS IN

○ What is the German for where? _____

○ What is the German for what? _____

○ What is the German for how? _____

○ What is the German for who? _____

○ What is the German for why? _____

TURN BACK FOR THE ANSWERS

Now cover up the answers below and translate the following:

(You can write your answers in)

1. WHERE IS THE RESTAURANT?
2. WHY IS SHE HERE?
3. HOW WAS THE SPOON?
4. WHAT IS IT?
5. WHO IS THE WAITER?

The answers are:

1. WO IST DAS RESTAURANT?
2. WARUM IST SIE HIER?
3. WIE WAR DER LÖFFEL?
4. WAS IST ES?
5. WER IST DER OBER?

Now cover up the answers below and translate the following:

(You can write your answers in)

1. WAS IST DAS?
2. WER IST DIE MUTTER?
3. WARUM WAR DIE GANS DA?
4. WO IST ER, UND WO IST SIE?
5. WIE VIEL IST ES?

The answers are:

1. WHAT IS THAT?
2. WHO IS THE MOTHER?
3. WHY WAS THE GOOSE THERE?
4. WHERE IS HE, AND WHERE IS SHE?
5. HOW MUCH IS IT?

ELEMENTARY GRAMMAR: Plurals

Because plurals are very complicated in German, you will now be given a few simple rules which will be correct in the majority of cases.

Don't worry about being wrong, however, as you will still be understood even if you make a mistake.

The FIRST rule is that the word for THE is always DIE when the noun is plural — whether the noun is masculine, feminine or neuter.

So,

THE DOGS	is	DIE HUNDE
THE CATS	is	DIE KATZEN
THE KNIVES	is	DIE MESSER

The SECOND rule is this: for MASCULINE and NEUTER nouns, if the word is short add an "E" at the end to make it plural. If it is a long word, leave it alone.

So,

DER HUND	is	THE DOG
DIE HUNDE	is	THE DOGS

but

DER TELLER	is	THE PLATE
DIE TELLER	is	THE PLATES

The THIRD rule is this: if the word is FEMININE, make it end with "EN" in the plural.

So,

DIE KATZE	is	THE CAT
DIE KATZEN	is	THE CATS

As was said at the beginning, you will make mistakes using these rules but you will always be understood — and you will usually be right in any case.

To summarise:

For FEMININE words, make sure the words end in "EN" in the plural. For example, DIE KATZEN, DIE FLASCHEN.

For MASCULINE and NEUTER words:

If the word is short — add an "E" to make it plural. For example, DIE HUNDE.

If the word is long — leave it alone. For example, DIE TELLER.

Now cover up the answers below and translate the following:

(You can write your answers in)

1. THE PLATES ARE VERY HEAVY
2. THE CATS ARE WHITE
3. THE DOGS ARE LATE
4. THE TABLES ARE BIG
5. THE CUPS AND THE SAUCERS ARE VERY WHITE

The answers are:

1. DIE TELLER SIND SEHR SCHWER
2. DIE KATZEN SIND WEISS
3. DIE HUNDE SIND SPÄT
4. DIE TISCHE SIND GROSS
5. DIE TASSEN UND DIE UNTERTASSEN SIND SEHR WEISS

Now cover up the answers below and translate the following:

(You can write your answers in)

1. DIE UNTERTASSEN SIND GROSS
2. DIE FLASCHEN SIND WEISS
3. DIE SCHWEINE UND DIE HUMMER SIND SEHR ROT
4. DIE MÄDCHEN SIND SCHWER
5. DIE RASEN UND DIE GARDINEN SIND SCHWARZ

The answers are:

1. THE SAUCERS ARE BIG
2. THE BOTTLES ARE WHITE
3. THE PIGS AND THE LOBSTERS ARE VERY RED
4. THE GIRLS ARE HEAVY
5. THE LAWNS AND THE CURTAINS ARE BLACK

FOOD AND DRINK

THINK OF EACH IMAGE IN YOUR MIND'S EYE FOR ABOUT TEN SECONDS

○ The German for MEAT is FLEISCH   (FLISH)*
  Imagine eating raw FLESH for meat.

○ The German for COFFEE is KAFFEE   (KAFAY)
  Imagine drinking coffee in a CAFE.

○ The German for TEA is TEE   (TAY)
  Imagine spilling TEA on the German flag.

○ The German for CAKE is KUCHEN   (KOOCHEN)
  Imagine COOKING beautiful cakes.

○ The German for CREAM is SAHNE   (ZAHNE)
  Imagine dropping SAND into your cream.

○ The German for SALAD is SALAT   (ZALAT)
  Imagine spilling SALAD all over the German flag.

○ The German for MENU is   (SHPIZEHKARTEH)*
  SPEISEKARTE
  Imagine spies in a restaurant
  disguising their secrets so they look
  like menus, they are SPIES CARDS.

○ The German for SOUP is SUPPE   (ZUPPEH)*
  Imagine spilling SOUP on a German flag.

○ The German for FRUIT is OBST   (OHBST)
  Imagine someone who HOPES TO grow fruit.

○ The German for CHICKEN is HUHN   (HOOHN)
  Imagine asking "WHO NOW wants chicken?"

* The I is pronounced like the I in "wine", the U like the U in "put".

103

YOU CAN WRITE YOUR ANSWERS IN

○ What is the English for Huhn? _____

○ What is the English for Obst? _____

○ What is the English for Suppe? _____

○ What is the English for Speisekarte? _____

○ What is the English for Salat? _____

○ What is the English for Sahne? _____

○ What is the English for Kuchen? _____

○ What is the English for Tee? _____

○ What is the English for Kaffee? _____

○ What is the English for Fleisch? _____

TURN BACK FOR THE ANSWERS

GENDERS

**THINK OF EACH IMAGE IN YOUR MIND'S EYE FOR
ABOUT TEN SECONDS**

○ The gender of MEAT is Neuter: DAS FLEISCH
  Imagine heating meat over a fire.

○ The gender of COFFEE is Masculine: DER KAFFEE
  Imagine a boxer drinking a cup of coffee between rounds.

○ The gender of TEA is Masculine: DER TEE
  Imagine a boxer drinking tea between rounds.

○ The gender of CAKE is Masculine: DER KUCHEN
  Imagine a boxer baking a cake with his gloves on.

○ The gender of CREAM is Feminine: DIE SAHNE
  Imagine a beautiful little girl eating a bowl of whipped cream.

○ The gender of SALAD is Masculine: DER SALAT
  Imagine a boxer trying to diet on green salad.

○ The gender of MENU is Feminine: DIE SPEISEKARTE
  Imagine a little girl trying to choose something from the menu.

○ The gender of SOUP is Feminine: DIE SUPPE
  Imagine a little girl spilling soup all down her pretty dress.

○ The gender of FRUIT is Neuter: DAS OBST
  Imagine throwing fruit on to the fire.

○ The gender of CHICKEN is Neuter: DAS HUHN
  Imagine roasting a chicken over the fire.

YOU CAN WRITE YOUR ANSWERS IN

○ What is the gender and German for chicken? _____

○ What is the gender and German for fruit? _____

○ What is the gender and German for soup? _____

○ What is the gender and German for menu? _____

○ What is the gender and German for salad? _____

○ What is the gender and German for cream? _____

○ What is the gender and German for cake? _____

○ What is the gender and German for tea? _____

○ What is the gender and German for coffee? _____

○ What is the gender and German for meat? _____

TURN BACK FOR THE ANSWERS

NUMBERS

THINK OF EACH IMAGE IN YOUR MIND'S EYE FOR ABOUT TEN SECONDS

○ The German for ONE is EINS   (INS)*
  Imagine ONE tin of HEINZ baked beans.

○ The German for TWO is ZWEI   (TSVI)*
  Imagine thinking, "WHY TWO?"

○ The German for THREE is DREI   (DRI)*
  Imagine seeing THREE shirts DRYing on the line.

○ The German for FOUR is VIER   (FEER)
  Imagine you FEAR the number FOUR.

○ The German for FIVE is FÜNF   (FOONF)
  Imagine thinking, "FIVE is FUN."

○ The German for SIX is SECHS   (ZEX)
  Imagine SIX German flags.

○ The German for SEVEN is SIEBEN   (ZEEBEN)
  Imagine SEVEN German flags, one for each of
  the SEVEN deadly sins.

○ The German for EIGHT is ACHT   (ACHT)
  Imagine you ACT in a play which starts at
  EIGHT o'clock.

○ The German for NINE is NEUN   (NOIN)
  Imagine waving German flags as you listen to the
  NINE o'clock News.

○ The German for TEN is ZEHN   (TSAIN)
  Imagine someone asking if you are SANE to visit
  TEN Downing Street.

* The I is pronounced like the I in "wine".

YOU CAN WRITE YOUR ANSWERS IN

○ What is the English for zehn? _____

○ What is the English for neun? _____

○ What is the English for acht? _____

○ What is the English for sieben? _____

○ What is the English for sechs? _____

○ What is the English for fünf? _____

○ What is the English for vier? _____

○ What is the English for drei? _____

○ What is the English for zwei? _____

○ What is the English for eins? _____

TURN BACK FOR THE ANSWERS

YOU CAN WRITE YOUR ANSWERS IN

○ **What is the German for ten?** _____

○ **What is the German for nine?** _____

○ **What is the German for eight?** _____

○ **What is the German for seven?** _____

○ **What is the German for six?** _____

○ **What is the German for five?** _____

○ **What is the German for four?** _____

○ **What is the German for three?** _____

○ **What is the German for two?** _____

○ **What is the German for one?** _____

TURN BACK FOR THE ANSWERS

Now cover up the answers below and translate the following:

(You can write your answers in)

1. THE MEAT IS VERY RED, BUT FIVE PLATES ARE WHITE
2. WHERE IS THE COFFEE, AND WHERE IS THE CREAM?
3. NO, THE SOUP IS NOT GOOD, BUT NINE CUPS ARE GOOD
4. WHY IS THE CAKE BLUE, AND WHY ARE THREE MENUS GREEN?
5. THE SALAD IS VERY BAD AND THE CHICKEN IS ALSO BAD

The answers are:

1. DAS FLEISCH IST SEHR ROT, ABER FÜNF TELLER SIND WEISS
2. WO IST DER KAFFEE, UND WO IST DIE SAHNE?
3. NEIN, DIE SUPPE IST NICHT GUT, ABER NEUN TASSEN SIND GUT
4. WARUM IST DER KUCHEN BLAU, UND WARUM SIND DREI SPEISEKARTEN GRÜN?
5. DER SALAT IST SEHR SCHLECHT, UND DAS HUHN IST AUCH SCHLECHT

Now cover up the answers below and translate the following:

(You can write your answers in)

1. ZWEI FLASCHEN UND DREI TELLER SIND SCHWER
2. VIER MESSER UND SECHS LÖFFEL SIND GUT
3. DA SIND SIEBEN TISCHE UND ACHT MÄDCHEN
4. WARUM IST DER OBER SCHLECHT?
5. DAS RESTAURANT IST IMMER SEHR GUT

The answers are:

1. TWO BOTTLES AND THREE PLATES ARE HEAVY
2. FOUR KNIVES AND SIX SPOONS ARE GOOD
3. THERE ARE SEVEN TABLES AND EIGHT GIRLS
4. WHY IS THE WAITER BAD?
5. THE RESTAURANT IS ALWAYS VERY GOOD

TELLING THE TIME

In order to tell the time in German you will first need to know a few more words.

THINK OF EACH IMAGE IN YOUR MIND'S EYE FOR ABOUT TEN SECONDS

○ The German for ELEVEN is ELF   (ELF)
   Imagine ELEVEN ELFS playing football.

○ The German for TWELVE is ZWÖLF   (TSVE(r)LF)
   Imagine TWELVE rolls SWELL when you bake them.

○ The German for TWENTY is ZWANZIG   (TSVANTSICH)
   Imagine seeing TWENTY SWANS SICK.

○ The German for TWENTY-FIVE is
   FÜNFUNDZWANZIG   (FOONFUNTTSVANTSICH)
   Imagine you add FIVE AND TWENTY
   together to give TWENTY-FIVE.

○ The German for QUARTER is VIERTEL   (FEERTEL)
   Imagine a FERTILE QUARTER of a field.

○ The German for HALF is HALB   (HALB)
   Imagine shouting "HELP he has cut the lady in HALF."

○ The German for AFTER is NACH   (NACH)
   Imagine someone who has the KNACK
   of arriving AFTER everybody has gone.

○ The German for BEFORE is VOR   (FOR)
   Imagine shouting "FOUR!"
   BEFORE hitting the ball at golf.

YOU CAN WRITE YOUR ANSWERS IN

○ What is the English for vor?   _____

○ What is the English for nach?   _____

○ What is the English for halb?   _____

○ What is the English for viertel?   _____

○ What is the English for fünfundzwanzig?   _____

○ What is the English for zwanzig?   _____

○ What is the English for zwölf?   _____

○ What is the English for elf?   _____

TURN BACK FOR THE ANSWERS

YOU CAN WRITE YOUR ANSWERS IN

○ What is the German for eleven?   _____

○ What is the German for twelve?   _____

○ What is the German for twenty?   _____

○ What is the German for twenty-five?   _____

○ What is the German for quarter?   _____

○ What is the German for half?   _____

○ What is the German for after?   _____

○ What is the German for before?   _____

TURN BACK FOR THE ANSWERS

TELLING THE TIME

To ask the time in German you ask:

HOW MUCH CLOCK IS IT?

In German this is:

WIE VIEL UHR IST ES?

To say   IT IS TWO O'CLOCK you say IT IS TWO CLOCK
                                       or ES IST ZWEI UHR

To say   IT IS FIVE O'CLOCK you say ES IST FÜNF UHR

To say IT IS FIVE PAST TWO or IT IS TEN PAST THREE
you say IT IS FIVE *AFTER* TWO or IT IS TEN *AFTER* THREE

In German this is:

ES IST FÜNF *NACH* ZWEI or ES IST ZEHN *NACH* DREI

To say IT IS QUARTER PAST FOUR you say IT IS
                                            QUARTER
                                            AFTER FOUR

In German this is:

ES IST VIERTEL NACH VIER

To say   IT IS TEN TO FIVE   or FIVE TO SIX
you say IT IS TEN *BEFORE* FIVE or FIVE *BEFORE* SIX

In German this is:

ES IST ZEHN *VOR* FÜNF or ES IST FÜNF *VOR* SECHS

To say IT IS QUARTER TO FIVE you say ES IST VIERTEL
                                            VOR FÜNF

The only tricky time is half past the hour.

To say IT IS HALF PAST EIGHT you say IT IS HALF NINE

In German this is:

ES IST HALB NEUN

In other words, the Germans take half of an hour FROM THE
NEXT hour.

So,

HALB ZEHN   is HALF PAST NINE

HALB ZWÖLF is HALF PAST ELEVEN

and so on.

116

Now cover up the answers below and translate the following:

(You can write your answers in)

1. IT IS QUARTER PAST TWELVE
2. IT IS TWENTY TO ELEVEN
3. IT IS TWENTY-FIVE PAST SIX
4. IT IS HALF PAST FOUR
5. IT IS QUARTER TO THREE
6. IT IS TWENTY-FIVE TO SEVEN

The answers are:

1. ES IST VIERTEL NACH ZWÖLF
2. ES IST ZWANZIG VOR ELF
3. ES IST FÜNFUNDZWANZIG NACH SECHS
4. ES IST HALB FÜNF
5. ES IST VIERTEL VOR DREI
6. ES IST FÜNFUNDZWANZIG VOR SIEBEN

Section 6 FOOD AND DRINK

THINK OF EACH IMAGE IN YOUR MIND'S EYE FOR ABOUT TEN SECONDS

○ The German for EGG is EI   (I)*
Imagine an EYE painted on the shell of an egg.

○ The German for BACON is SPECK   (SHPEK)
Imagine tiny SPECKS all over your bacon.

○ The German for BREAD is BROT   (BROHT)
Imagine a BROAD loaf of bread which
spreads all over the table.

○ The German for BUTTER is BUTTER   (BUTER)*
Imagine BUTTER spread all over the German flag.

○ The German for JAM is MARMELADE (MARMELAHDEH)
Imagine MARMALADE mixed with
strawberry and plum jam.

○ The German for SAUSAGE is WURST   (VURST)*
Imagine eating the WORST sausage
you have ever tasted, and spitting it out.

○ The German for CHEESE is KÄSE   (KAISEH)
Imagine a CASE filled with a whole lot of different cheeses.

○ The German for WATER is WASSER   (VASSER)
Imagine a glass of WATER on the German flag.

○ The German for WINE is WEIN   (VINE)
Imagine a VINE with bottles of wine
hanging down instead of grapes.

○ The German for MILK is MILCH   (MILCH)
Imagine a bottle of MILK standing at
your door on a German flag.

* The I is pronounced like the I in "wine", the U like the U in "put".

YOU CAN WRITE YOUR ANSWERS IN

○ What is the English for Milch? _____

○ What is the English for Wein? _____

○ What is the English for Wasser? _____

○ What is the English for Käse? _____

○ What is the English for Wurst? _____

○ What is the English for Marmelade? _____

○ What is the English for Butter? _____

○ What is the English for Brot? _____

○ What is the English for Speck? _____

○ What is the English for Ei? _____

TURN BACK FOR THE ANSWERS

GENDERS

THINK OF EACH IMAGE IN YOUR MIND'S EYE FOR ABOUT TEN SECONDS

○ The gender of EGG is Neuter: DAS EI
Imagine cooking an egg over a fire.

○ The gender of BACON is Masculine: DER SPECK
Imagine a boxer tucking into a plate of bacon.

○ The gender of BREAD is Neuter: DAS BROT
Imagine throwing stale bread on to a fire.

○ The gender of BUTTER is Feminine: DIE BUTTER
Imagine a little girl carrying packs of butter.

○ The gender of JAM is Feminine: DIE MARMELADE
Imagine a little girl spreading thick
strawberry jam all over her face.

○ The gender of SAUSAGE is Feminine: DIE WURST
Imagine a little girl tucking into a huge jumbo sausage.

○ The gender of CHEESE is Masculine: DER KÄSE
Imagine a boxer holding lumps of cheese in his boxing gloves.

○ The gender of WATER is Neuter: DAS WASSER
Imagine pouring water on to a fire to put it out.

○ The gender of WINE is Masculine: DER WEIN
Imagine a boxer drinking a bottle of
wine between rounds and getting tipsy.

○ The gender of MILK is Feminine: DIE MILCH
Imagine a little girl drinking from a bottle of milk.

YOU CAN WRITE YOUR ANSWERS IN

○ **What is the gender and German for milk?** _____

○ **What is the gender and German for wine?** _____

○ **What is the gender and German for water?** _____

○ **What is the gender and German for cheese?** _____

○ **What is the gender and German for sausage?** _____

○ **What is the gender and German for jam?** _____

○ **What is the gender and German for butter?** _____

○ **What is the gender and German for bread?** _____

○ **What is the gender and German for bacon?** _____

○ **What is the gender and German for egg?** _____

TURN BACK FOR THE ANSWERS

SOME MORE FOOD AND DRINK WORDS

THINK OF EACH IMAGE IN YOUR MIND'S EYE FOR ABOUT TEN SECONDS

○ The German for CABBAGE is KOHL   (KOHL)
Imagine a huge pile of COAL with cabbages
growing out of the top.

○ The German for BEAN is BOHNE   (BONEH)
Imagine a BONE covered in baked beans.

○ The German for TOMATO is TOMATE   (TOMAHTEH)
Imagine a TOMATO that has been squashed
into the German flag.

○ The German for PEA is ERBSE   (ERBSEH)
Imagine a plate of peas with mixed HERBS
mixed in with them.

○ The German for ONION is ZWIEBEL   (TSVEEBEL)
Imagine a WEE BELL in the shape of an
onion. When you pick it up the bell smells of onion.

○ The German for POTATO is KARTOFFEL   (KARTOFFEL)
Imagine someone CARTING OFF a huge
load of potatoes. Imagine some of the
potatoes falling off the cart.

○ The German for VEGETABLE is GEMÜSE   (GEMOOZEH)
Imagine a cook AMUSING people by
cutting vegetables in funny shapes. Imagine
people laughing as he does so.

○ The German for MUSHROOM is PILZ   (PILTS)
Imagine the doctor giving you large PILLS
which taste and feel like mushrooms.

○ The German for PEAR is BIRNE   (BIRNEH)
Imagine BURNING a pear.

○ The German for APPLE is APFEL   (APFEL)
Imagine an APPLE on the German flag.

YOU CAN WRITE YOUR ANSWERS IN

○ What is the English for Apfel? _____

○ What is the English for Birne? _____

○ What is the English for Pilz? _____

○ What is the English for Gemüse? _____

○ What is the English for Kartoffel? _____

○ What is the English for Zwiebel? _____

○ What is the English for Erbse? _____

○ What is the English for Tomate? _____

○ What is the English for Bohne? _____

○ What is the English for Kohl? _____

TURN BACK FOR THE ANSWERS

GENDERS

THINK OF EACH IMAGE IN YOUR MIND'S EYE FOR ABOUT TEN SECONDS

○ The gender of CABBAGE is Masculine: DER KOHL
Imagine a boxer throwing a cabbage at his opponent.

○ The gender of BEAN is Feminine: DIE BOHNE
Imagine a little girl tucking into a plate full of baked beans.

○ The gender of TOMATO is Feminine: DIE TOMATE
Imagine a mighty little girl squashing tomatoes with her shoe.

○ The gender of PEA is Feminine: DIE ERBSE
Imagine a little girl firing a pea through a pea shooter.

○ The gender of ONION is Feminine: DIE ZWIEBEL
Imagine a little girl crying as she peels onions.

○ The gender of POTATO is Feminine: DIE KARTOFFEL
Imagine a little girl helping mum to peel a large bowl of potatoes.

○ The gender of VEGETABLE is Neuter: DAS GEMÜSE
Imagine a fire being pelted with all sorts of vegetables.

○ The gender of MUSHROOM is Masculine: DER PILZ
Imagine a boxer eating a magic mushroom because he thinks it will give him extra strength.

○ The gender of PEAR is Feminine: DIE BIRNE
Imagine a little girl with a large pear.

○ The gender of APPLE is Masculine: DER APFEL
Imagine a boxer with a large apple in his mouth to stop his teeth being knocked out.

YOU CAN WRITE YOUR ANSWERS IN

○ What is the gender and German for apple? _____

○ What is the gender and German for pear? _____

○ What is the gender and German for mushroom? _____

○ What is the gender and German for vegetable? _____

○ What is the gender and German for potato? _____

○ What is the gender and German for onion? _____

○ What is the gender and German for pea? _____

○ What is the gender and German for tomato? _____

○ What is the gender and German for bean? _____

○ What is the gender and German for cabbage? _____

TURN BACK FOR THE ANSWERS

SOME COMMON WORDS USED WITH "ICH"

THINK OF EACH IMAGE IN YOUR MIND'S EYE FOR ABOUT TEN SECONDS

○ The German for LOVE is LIEBE   (LEEBEH)
 Imagine you LEAP into the arms of the one you LOVE.

○ The German for GIVE is GEBE   (GAIBEH)
 Imagine someone GIBBERing away: "GIVE me, give me."

○ The German for TAKE is NEHME   (NAIMEH)
 Imagine a policeman who wants to TAKE your NAME.

○ The German for DO is TUE   (TOO EH)
 Imagine saying, "I DO TOO."

○ The German for EAT is ESSE   (ESSEH)
 Imagine saying, "YES SIR, I want to EAT."

○ The German for GO is GEHE   (GAI EH)
 Imagine GOING GAY.

○ The German for HAVE is HABE   (HAHBEH)
 Imagine I HAVE a HARBOUR.

○ The German for MAKE is MACHE   (MACHEH)
 Imagine you MAKE a German flag.

PLEASE NOTE

In German you often use MACHE for DO, instead of TUE.

For example, I DO IT is ICH MACHE ES

YOU CAN WRITE YOUR ANSWERS IN

○ What is the English for mache? _____

○ What is the English for habe? _____

○ What is the English for gehe? _____

○ What is the English for esse? _____

○ What is the English for tue? _____

○ What is the English for nehme? _____

○ What is the English for gebe? _____

○ What is the English for liebe? _____

TURN BACK FOR THE ANSWERS

128

YOU CAN WRITE YOUR ANSWERS IN

○ What is the German for make? _____

○ What is the German for have? _____

○ What is the German for go? _____

○ What is the German for eat? _____

○ What is the German for do? _____

○ What is the German for take? _____

○ What is the German for give? _____

○ What is the German for love? _____

TURN BACK FOR THE ANSWERS

ELEMENTARY GRAMMAR

The words you have just been given end in "e" when they are used with the word "I".

So,

> I GO (or I AM GOING)   is ICH GEHE
>
> I LOVE (or I AM LOVING) is ICH LIEBE

For example,

> I LOVE IT   is ICH LIEB*E* ES
>
> I AM DOING IT is ICH TU*E* ES

If, however, you want to say YOU — using SIE for you — then:

> YOU GO   is SIE GEH*EN*
>
> YOU HAVE is SIE HAB*EN*

In other words, you add EN to the end of the word. For example,

> YOU HAVE THAT is SIE HAB*EN* DAS

If you want to say, for example, "The dog and the cat HAVE it", you also use the word HABEN.

So,

THE DOG AND THE CAT HAVE IT is DER HUND UND DIE
KATZE HAB*EN* ES

THE DOG AND THE CAT LOVE IT is DER HUND UND DIE
KATZE LIEB*EN* ES

Also,

> THEY DO IT   is SIE TU*EN* ES
>
> THEY MAKE IT is SIE MACH*EN* ES

N.B. TUEN is often written as TUN

Please note, also, that the word SIE in German can mean THEY, as well as YOU and SHE.

Now cover up the answers below and translate the following:

(You can write your answers in)

1. THE GOOSE AND THE DUCK LOVE IT
2. YOU MAKE IT (not to a friend)
3. I GO THERE
4. YOU AND I HAVE IT (not to a friend)
5. THE BREAD AND THE JAM DO IT

The answers are:

1. DIE GANS UND DIE ENTE LIEBEN ES
2. SIE MACHEN ES
3. ICH GEHE DA HIN (note the HIN — the German for "go there" is "hin gehen")
4. SIE UND ICH HABEN ES
5. DAS BROT UND DIE MARMELADE TUN ES

Now cover up the answers below and translate the following:

(You can write your answers in)

1. ICH ESSE HIER
2. DER HUND UND DIE KATZE LIEBEN ES
3. DAS PFERD UND DIE MAUS MACHEN ES
4. DER APFEL UND DIE BIRNEN HABEN ES
5. SIE LIEBEN ES

The answers are:

1. I EAT HERE
2. THE DOG AND THE CAT LOVE IT
3. THE HORSE AND THE MOUSE MAKE IT
4. THE APPLE AND THE PEARS HAVE IT
5. YOU LOVE IT

ELEMENTARY GRAMMAR: A and AN

The German for A or AN — as in A DOG or AN APPLE — is EIN (the "EI" part of the word is pronounced like "eye"). EIN is pronounced as in Albert EINstein.

For MASCULINE and NEUTER words,

A is EIN, as in:

EIN HUND   for A DOG

EIN APFEL   for AN APPLE

EIN SCHWEIN for A PIG

For FEMININE words, EIN has an "e" on the end to make EIN*E*. This extra "e" is pronounced like the "e" in "hen".

So,

EIN*E* FRAU   is A WIFE

EIN*E* KATZE is A CAT

So,

EIN HUND UND EINE KATZE SIND LAUT is A DOG AND
A CAT ARE NOISY

Now cover up the answers below and translate the following:

(You can write your answers in)

1. A PEAR AND AN APPLE ARE BROWN
2. A POTATO AND AN ONION ARE VERY BIG
3. A CABBAGE AND A BEAN ARE ONLY GREEN
4. A MUSHROOM IS VERY WHITE
5. AN EGG AND A SAUSAGE ARE HERE

The answers are:

1. EINE BIRNE UND EIN APFEL SIND BRAUN
2. EINE KARTOFFEL UND EINE ZWIEBEL SIND SEHR GROSS
3. EIN KOHL UND EINE BOHNE SIND NUR GRÜN
4. EIN PILZ IST SEHR WEISS
5. EIN EI UND EINE WURST SIND HIER

Now cover up the answers below and translate the following:

(You can write your answers in)

1. EIN EI IST GUT
2. EINE WURST IST GROSS
3. EINE SPINNE IST SCHNELL
4. EIN KOHL IST GRÜN
5. EINE ZWIEBEL IST ROT

The answers are:

1. AN EGG IS GOOD
2. A SAUSAGE IS BIG
3. A SPIDER IS QUICK
4. A CABBAGE IS GREEN
5. AN ONION IS RED

ELEMENTARY GRAMMAR

If you want to say "He does something or other", for example, HE LOVES A DOG or YOU LOVE A CAT, then the word for "a" is exactly the same as in the previous section:

EIN for a neuter word, and EINE for a feminine word.

For feminine:

I EAT A CAT has the same ending on ein(e):

ICH ESSE EINE KATZE

For neuter:

I EAT A PIG has the same ending on ein (ein):

ICH ESSE EIN SCHWEIN

But if the word is masculine then EIN ends in EN.

So,

I EAT A DOG is ICH ESSE EINEN HUND

In summary:

NEUTER
I HAVE A PIG   is ICH HABE EIN SCHWEIN

FEMININE
YOU HAVE A COW is SIE HABEN EINE KUH

MASCULINE
YOU GIVE A DOG   is SIE GEBEN EINEN HUND

The words DOG, PIG and CAT in the sentences above are the objects of the sentence.

To tell whether a word is the object of a sentence is very simple.

If a word is having something done to it, it is the object of the sentence.

So, being loved, eated, had, called, taken, given, and so on, means that the word coming after is the object of the sentence.

136

So,

    I HAVE A DOG
    I LOVE A DOG
    HE EATS A DOG
    SHE GIVES A DOG

all mean that A DOG is the object of the sentence.

    I HAVE A DOG is ICH HABE EIN*EN* HUND

The only exception to worry about just now is the word IS. For this word you simply stick to the endings you used before.

So,

    IT IS A DOG is ES IST EIN HUND
    IT IS A CAT is ES IST EIN*E* KATZE

You must not worry about this. You can only make a mistake for masculine words. In any case, you will be understood even if you do make a mistake.

Now cover up the answers below and translate the following:

(You can write your answers in)

1. I HAVE A TOMATO, AN APPLE AND A PEAR
2. YOU LOVE BACON, AN EGG AND BEANS (not to a friend)
3. THE BREAD, THE BUTTER AND THE JAM ARE VERY GOOD, BUT VERY HEAVY
4. I LOVE IT HERE
5. THE WATER IS GOOD AND THE CHEESE IS ALWAYS RED

The answers are:

1. ICH HABE EINE TOMATE, EINEN APFEL UND EINE BIRNE
2. SIE LIEBEN SPECK, EIN EI UND BOHNEN
3. DAS BROT, DIE BUTTER UND DIE MARMELADE SIND SEHR GUT, ABER SEHR SCHWER
4. ICH LIEBE ES HIER
5. DAS WASSER IST GUT, UND DER KÄSE IST IMMER ROT

Now cover up the answers below and translate the following:

(You can write your answers in)

1. ICH LIEBE EINE SPINNE, UND ICH HABE EINE ENTE

2. ICH MACHE EINE BLUSE, UND ICH MACHE EINEN ROCK

3. ICH LIEBE EIN BETT, ABER ICH MACHE EIN BRETT

4. SIE MACHEN EINEN TEPPICH, ABER ICH MACHE EINE GARDINE

5. ICH ESSE ZWEI KARTOFFELN, UND SIE ESSEN VIER BOHNEN

The answers are:

1. I LOVE A SPIDER, AND I HAVE A DUCK

2. I AM MAKING A BLOUSE, AND I AM MAKING A SKIRT

3. I LOVE A BED, BUT I AM MAKING A SHELF

4. YOU ARE MAKING A CARPET, BUT I AM MAKING A CURTAIN

5. I AM EATING TWO POTATOES, AND YOU ARE EATING FOUR BEANS

Now cover up the answers below and translate the following:

(You can write your answers in)

1. I LOVE A CABBAGE
2. YOU MAKE A CUPBOARD
3. I HAVE A SAUSAGE, YOU HAVE NINE TOMATOES
4. I DO IT
5. THE WINE AND THE MILK ARE VERY BAD

The answers are:

1. ICH LIEBE EINEN KOHL
2. SIE MACHEN EINEN SCHRANK
3. ICH HABE EINE WURST, SIE HABEN NEUN TOMATEN
4. ICH TUE ES
5. DER WEIN UND DIE MILCH SIND SEHR SCHLECHT

Section 7   SHOPPING AND BUSINESS WORDS

THINK OF EACH IMAGE IN YOUR MIND'S EYE FOR ABOUT TEN SECONDS

O The German for WORKER is ARBEITER   (ARBITER)*
Imagine selecting HARD BITERS as your workers.

O The German for PROFESSION is BERUF   (BEROOF)
Imagine a meeting of professional men on the ROOF.

O The German for BOSS is CHEF   (SHEF)
Imagine your boss is a spare-time CHEF,
preparing meals for a restaurant.

O The German for TRADESMAN is HANDWERKER
Imagine a tradesman working with his   (HANTVERKER)
hands, a HANDWORKER.

O The German for OWNER is BESITZER   (BEZITSER)
Imagine the owner of a business lives BESIDE HER.

O The German for TRAINING is AUSBILDUNG
Imagine putting trainees to   (OWSBILDUNG)
HOUSE BUILDING.

O The German for FIRM is FIRMA   (FEERMA)
Imagine the FIRM you are visiting has the German flag
outside.

O The German for SALARY is GEHALT   (GEHALT)
Imagine your firm tries to HALT paying your salary.

O The German for PRODUCT is PRODUKT   (PRODUKT)
Imagine covering a number of
PRODUCTS with the German flag.

O The German for CHEQUE is SCHECK   (SHEK)
Imagine a CHEQUE book lying on the German flag.

* The I is pronounced like the I in "wine".

141

YOU CAN WRITE YOUR ANSWERS IN

○ What is the English for Scheck? _____

○ What is the English for Produkt? _____

○ What is the English for Gehalt? _____

○ What is the English for Firma? _____

○ What is the English for Ausbildung? _____

○ What is the English for Besitzer? _____

○ What is the English for Handwerker? _____

○ What is the English for Chef? _____

○ What is the English for Beruf? _____

○ What is the English for Arbeiter? _____

TURN BACK FOR THE ANSWERS

GENDERS

THINK OF EACH IMAGE IN YOUR MIND'S EYE FOR ABOUT TEN SECONDS

○ The gender of WORKER is Masculine: DER ARBEITER
Imagine a boxer working as a worker on a building site to build up his muscles. (A female worker is DIE ARBEITERIN and the gender is feminine.)

○ The gender of PROFESSION is Masculine: DER BERUF
Imagine a boxer punching members of the professions, one after the other: a doctor, a lawyer, and a teacher.

○ The gender of BOSS is Masculine: DER CHEF
Imagine a boxer trying his best at being a chef, with a chef's hat and boxing gloves. (A female boss is DIE CHEFIN.)

○ The gender of TRADESMAN is Masculine: DER HANDWERKER
Imagine a boxer keeping fit by working as a tradesman during the day.

○ The gender of OWNER is Masculine: DER BESITZER
Imagine a boxer who is the owner of a night club.

○ The gender of TRAINING is Feminine: DIE AUSBILDUNG
Imagine a little girl training very hard to become a nurse.

○ The gender of FIRM is Feminine: DIE FIRMA
Imagine a little girl going through the security gate of a large firm.

○ The gender of SALARY is Neuter: DAS GEHALT
Imagine putting your salary on a fire.

○ The gender of PRODUCT is Neuter: DAS PRODUKT
Imagine throwing products straight from a production line onto a fire.

○ The gender of CHEQUE is Masculine: DER SCHECK
Imagine a boxer being presented with a cheque after a fight.

YOU CAN WRITE YOUR ANSWERS IN

○ What is the gender and German for cheque? _____

○ What is the gender and German for product? _____

○ What is the gender and German for salary? _____

○ What is the gender and German for firm? _____

○ What is the gender and German for training? _____

○ What is the gender and German for owner? _____

○ What is the gender and German for tradesman? _____

○ What is the gender and German for boss? _____

○ What is the gender and German for profession? _____

○ What is the gender and German for worker? _____

REMEMBER The word for a female worker is "die Arbeiterin", and the gender is female.

REMEMBER The word for a female boss is "die Chefin" and the gender is female.

TURN BACK FOR THE ANSWERS

MORE BUSINESS WORDS

THINK OF EACH IMAGE IN YOUR MIND'S EYE FOR ABOUT TEN SECONDS

○ The German for RECEIPT is QUITTUNG　　　(QVITTUNG)
Imagine saying "I'm QUITTING if I don't get a receipt."

○ The German for THING is SACHE　　　(SACHEH)
Imagine putting a whole lot of different things in SACKS.

○ The German for FACTORY is FABRIK　　　(FABREEK)
Imagine FABRICS of different kinds being made in a factory.

○ The German for HOLIDAYS is FERIEN　　　(FAIRYEN)
Imagine FAIRIES getting ready to go off on holiday.

○ The German for PRICE is PREIS　　　(PRISE)
Imagine asking for the PRICE of a German flag.

○ The German for MISTAKE is FEHLER　　　(FAILER)
Imagine being told, "FAIL HER, she has made a mistake."

○ The German for MANAGER is LEITER　　　(LITER)*
Imagine giving a LIGHTER as a present to the manager.

○ The German for MARKET is MARKT　　　(MARKT)
Imagine goods being MARKED to go to market.

○ The German for CASH TILL is KASSE　　　(KASSEH)
Imagine CASH being put in the till.

○ The German for OFFICE is BÜRO　　　(BOOROH)
Imagine an old-fashioned writing BUREAU in your office.

The I is pronounced like the I in "wine".

YOU CAN WRITE YOUR ANSWERS IN

○ What is the English for Büro?   _____

○ What is the English for Kasse?   _____

○ What is the English for Markt?   _____

○ What is the English for Leiter?   _____

○ What is the English for Fehler?   _____

○ What is the English for Preis?   _____

○ What is the English for Ferien?   _____

○ What is the English for Fabrik?   _____

○ What is the English for Sache?   _____

○ What is the English for Quittung?   _____

TURN BACK FOR THE ANSWERS

GENDERS

THINK OF EACH IMAGE IN YOUR MIND'S EYE FOR ABOUT TEN SECONDS

○ The gender of RECEIPT is Feminine: DIE QUITTUNG
  Imagine a little girl writing on a receipt
  for a doll she has just bought.

○ The gender of THING is Feminine: DIE SACHE
  Imagine a little girl playing with lots of different things.

○ The gender of FACTORY is Feminine: DIE FABRIK
  Imagine a little girl working hard in a dirty factory.

○ The gender of HOLIDAYS is Feminine: DIE FERIEN
  Imagine a little girl going off for her Summer holidays.
  (DIE FERIEN is, in fact, plural)

○ The gender of PRICE is Masculine: DER PREIS
  Imagine a boxer asking the price of his prize.

○ The gender of MISTAKE is Masculine: DER FEHLER
  Imagine a boxer making a big mistake
  and getting knocked out.

○ The gender of MANAGER is Masculine: DER LEITER
  Imagine a boxer's manager advising his boxer about a fight.

○ The gender of MARKET is Masculine: DER MARKT
  Imagine a boxer fighting a bout in a ring at the local market.

○ The gender of CASH TILL is Feminine: DIE KASSE
  Imagine a little girl trying to operate the cash till.

○ The gender of OFFICE is Neuter: DAS BÜRO
  Imagine a fire sweeping through an office.

YOU CAN WRITE YOUR ANSWERS IN

○ What is the gender and German for office? _____

○ What is the gender and German for cash till? _____

○ What is the gender and German for market? _____

○ What is the gender and German for manager? _____

○ What is the gender and German for mistake? _____

○ What is the gender and German for price? _____

○ What is the gender and German for holiday? _____

○ What is the gender and German for factory? _____

○ What is the gender and German for thing? _____

○ What is the gender and German for receipt? _____

TURN BACK FOR THE ANSWERS

SOME USEFUL WORDS

THINK OF EACH IMAGE IN YOUR MIND'S EYE FOR ABOUT TEN SECONDS

○ The German for PLEASE is BITTE   (BITTEH)
  Imagine feeling BITTER because
  someone did not say PLEASE nicely.

○ The German for THANKS is DANKE   (DANKEH)
  Imagine a little boy being put into a
  DANK dungeon because he would not say THANK YOU.

○ The German for OF COURSE is NATÜRLICH
  Imagine doing what comes NATURALLY,   (NATOORLICH)
  it comes as a matter OF COURSE, of course.

○ The German for FINE is SCHÖN   (SHE(r)N)
  Imagine a doctor who SHONE a torch
  into your eyes had pronounced them FINE.

○ The German for SORRY is ENTSCHULDIGUNG
  Imagine someone being SORRY that   (ENTSHULDIGUNG)*
  he was IN SCHOOL TOO YOUNG.

○ The German for SHORT is KURZ   (KURTS)
  Imagine someone being very CURT and SHORT with you.

○ The German for CHEAP is BILLIG   (BILLICH)
  Imagine buying a CHEAP BILLY Goat.

○ The German for DEAR (expensive) is TEUER   (TOIER)
  Imagine TIRING out an EXPENSIVE horse.

○ The German for NICE is NETT   (NETT)
  Imagine putting a NET over someone
  who is being NICE to you.

○ The German for NASTY is EKLIG   (EHKLICH)
  Imagine someone giving A CLICK
  every time he is about to be NASTY to you.

* The U is pronounced like the U in "put".

YOU CAN WRITE YOUR ANSWERS IN

○ What is the English for eklig? _____

○ What is the English for nett? _____

○ What is the English for teuer? _____

○ What is the English for billig? _____

○ What is the English for kurz? _____

○ What is the English for Entschuldigung? _____

○ What is the English for schön? _____

○ What is the English for natürlich? _____

○ What is the English for danke? _____

○ What is the English for bitte? _____

TURN BACK FOR THE ANSWERS

YOU CAN WRITE YOUR ANSWERS IN

○ What is the German for nasty? _____

○ What is the German for nice? _____

○ What is the German for dear (expensive)? _____

○ What is the German for cheap? _____

○ What is the German for short? _____

○ What is the German for sorry? _____

○ What is the German for fine? _____

○ What is the German for of course? _____

○ What is the German for thanks? _____

○ What is the German for please? _____

TURN BACK FOR THE ANSWERS

ELEMENTARY GRAMMAR

In the last section you learned that:

A DOG IS BIG is EIN HUND IST GROSS

A CAT IS BIG is EINE KATZE IST GROSS

A PIG IS BIG is EIN SCHWEIN IST GROSS

You also learned that:

I LOVE A DOG is ICH LIEBE EIN*EN* HUND

I LOVE A CAT is ICH LIEBE EIN*E* KATZE

I LOVE A PIG is ICH LIEBE EIN SCHWEIN

In this section we will look at the word THE.

You have already learned that the word "the" is:

DER if the noun is masculine — DER HUND IST MÜDE

DIE if the noun is feminine — DIE KATZE IST MÜDE

DAS if the noun is neuter — DAS SCHWEIN IST MÜDE

If you want to say I LOVE THE DOG or I LOVE THE CAT, etc., the word THE is DIE for feminine and DAS for neuter words as usual, but it becomes DEN for masculine words.

So,

I LOVE THE DOG is ICH LIEBE *DEN* HUND

I LOVE A DOG is ICH LIEBE EIN*EN* HUND

I LOVE THE CAT is ICH LIEBE *DIE* KATZE

I LOVE A CAT is ICH LIEBE EIN*E* KATZE

I LOVE THE PIG is ICH LIEBE *DAS* SCHWEIN

I LOVE A PIG is ICH LIEBE *EIN* SCHWEIN

In other words, the thing to remember is the word THE is only different in the masculine.

ICH LIEBE DEN HUND
ICH LIEBE EINEN HUND

REMEMBER that if you say IT IS THE DOG, then "is" is not a doing word.

So,

IT IS THE DOG is ES IST DER HUND

IT IS A DOG is ES IST EIN HUND

But do not worry if you don't get it right, you will still be understood.

Now cover up the answers below and translate the following:

(You can write your answers in)

1. OF COURSE I AM VERY TIRED, BUT THE OWNER IS A PIG
2. THE WORKER IS CHEAP, AND THE BOSS IS VERY NASTY
3. I LOVE THE FIRM, AND THE FACTORY IS NICE
4. THE RECEIPT IS NOT VERY BIG, AND I HAVE THE CHEQUE
5. IT IS A MISTAKE, BUT I LOVE THE CASH TILL

The answers are:

1. NATÜRLICH BIN ICH SEHR MÜDE, ABER DER BESITZER IST EIN SCHWEIN
2. DER ARBEITER IST BILLIG, UND DER CHEF IST SEHR EKLIG
3. ICH LIEBE DIE FIRMA, UND DIE FABRIK IST NETT
4. DIE QUITTUNG IST NICHT SEHR GROSS, UND ICH HABE DEN SCHECK
5. ES IST EIN FEHLER, ABER ICH LIEBE DIE KASSE

Now cover up the answers below and translate the following:

(You can write your answers in)

1. DIE FERIEN SIND SEHR KURZ
2. ICH HABE ZWEI SACHEN
3. WO SIND DIE KASSE UND DER SCHECK?
4. HEUTE WAR ES SEHR GUT
5. JA, ES IST DER BESITZER

The answers are:

1. THE HOLIDAYS ARE VERY SHORT
2. I HAVE TWO THINGS
3. WHERE ARE THE TILL AND THE CHEQUE?
4. TODAY IT WAS VERY GOOD
5. YES, IT IS THE OWNER

Now cover up the answers below and translate the following:

(You can write your answers in)

1. DIE AUSBILDUNG IST SEHR KURZ
2. DER BERUF IST SEHR SCHÖN, DANKE
3. DAS PRODUKT IST SEHR TEUER, ABER NATÜRLICH IST ES SEHR NETT
4. DIE FERIEN SIND SPÄT, UND DAS GEHALT IST SEHR SCHLECHT
5. WO IST DIE FABRIK, UND WO IST DER LEITER, BITTE?

The answers are:

1. THE TRAINING IS VERY SHORT
2. THE PROFESSION IS VERY FINE, THANKS
3. THE PRODUCT IS VERY DEAR, BUT OF COURSE IT IS VERY NICE
4. THE HOLIDAYS ARE LATE, AND THE SALARY IS VERY BAD
5. WHERE IS THE FACTORY, AND WHERE IS THE MANAGER, PLEASE?

SOME MORE ELEMENTARY GRAMMAR

You will remember that in an earlier section you learned that:

I HAVE (or am having)   is ICH HABE

YOU HAVE (or are having) is SIE HABEN

THE DOG AND THE CAT HAVE is also HABEN

If you want to say HE, or SHE or IT — LOVES, HAS, MAKES, etc., then:

HE HAS   is ER HA*T*

SHE LOVES is SIE LIEB*T*

In other words, the words end in "*t*"

For example,

SHE HAS IT is SIE HA*T* ES

HE DOES IT is ER TU*T* ES

If you want to use the word DU for YOU, then:

YOU HAVE is DU HA*ST*

YOU MAKE is DU MACH*ST*

In other words, the word ends in "*st*".

Now cover up the answers below and translate the following:

(You can write your answers in)

1. YOU HAVE A DOG (to a friend)
2. I LOVE A CAT
3. IT GOES
4. YOU MAKE A TABLE (to a friend)
5. THEY HAVE A MUSHROOM
6. SHE GOES

The answers are:

1. DU HAST EINEN HUND
2. ICH LIEBE EINE KATZE
3. ES GEHT
4. DU MACHST EINEN TISCH
5. SIE HABEN EINEN PILZ
6. SIE GEHT

Now cover up the answers below and translate the following:

(You can write your answers in)

1. DU HAST EINE KASSE
2. ER HAT EIN BÜRO
3. DER PREIS IST SEHR TEUER
4. DER MARKT IST BILLIG, UND DIE SACHEN SIND SEHR SCHÖN
5. ICH HABE EINEN SCHECK

The answers are:

1. YOU HAVE A CASH TILL
2. HE HAS AN OFFICE
3. THE PRICE IS VERY EXPENSIVE
4. THE MARKET IS CHEAP AND THE THINGS ARE VERY FINE
5. I HAVE A CHEQUE

Section 8 TRAVELLING, THE CAR

THINK OF EACH IMAGE IN YOUR MIND'S EYE FOR ABOUT TEN SECONDS

○ The German for PASSPORT is REISEPASS   (RIZEHPASS)*
Imagine sitting down with your passport
when an official shouts at you "RISE AND PASS."

○ The German for MONEY is GELD   (GELT)
Imagine feeling GUILTY because you have
no money to pay someone.

○ The German for SUITCASE is HANDKOFFER
Imagine someone sitting on a suitcase   (HANTKOFFER)
coughing through his hand — a HAND COUGHER.

○ The German for CUSTOMS is ZOLL   (TSOLL)
Imagine King SAUL from the Bible, spear
in hand, checking you at the customs.

○ The German for TOILET is TOILETTE   (TWALETTEH)
Imagine a TOILET with a German flag
draped over the toilet seat.

○ The German for GENTLEMEN is HERREN   (HERREN)
Imagine a huge HERRING dangling from
the door of the gentlemen's toilet.

○ The German for LADIES is DAMEN   (DAHMEN)
Imagine someone shouting at you
"DAMN AND blast" when you ask politely for
directions to the ladies.

○ The German for BUS is BUS   (BUS)*
Imagine a BUS draped with a large German flag.

○ The German for CAR is AUTO   (OWTOH)
Imagine a policeman yelling "OUT OH!" to
make you get out of your car.

○ The German for TRAIN is ZUG   (TSOOG)
Imagine you TOOK a train.

* The I is pronounced like the I in "wine", the U like the U in "put".

YOU CAN WRITE YOUR ANSWERS IN

○ What is the English for Zug?   _____

○ What is the English for Auto?   _____

○ What is the English for Bus?   _____

○ What is the English for Damen?   _____

○ What is the English for Herren?   _____

○ What is the English for Toilette?   _____

○ What is the English for Zoll?   _____

○ What is the English for Handkoffer?   _____

○ What is the English for Geld?   _____

○ What is the English for Reisepass?   _____

TURN BACK FOR THE ANSWERS

GENDERS

THINK OF EACH IMAGE IN YOUR MIND'S EYE FOR ABOUT TEN SECONDS

○ The gender of PASSPORT is Masculine: DER REISEPASS
Imagine a boxer being asked by the referee for his passport before he is allowed to fight.

○ The gender of MONEY is Neuter: DAS GELD
Imagine throwing piles of money onto a bonfire.

○ The gender of SUITCASE is Masculine: DER HANDKOFFER
Imagine a boxer putting his boxing gloves in a suitcase.

○ The gender of CUSTOMS is Masculine: DER ZOLL
Imagine a boxer punching a customs officer who challenges him.

○ The gender of TOILET is Feminine: DIE TOILETTE
Imagine a little girl sitting on a toilet seat.

○ The gender of GENTLEMEN is: DIE HERREN
Masculine plural

○ The gender of LADIES is Feminine plural: DIE DAMEN

○ The gender of BUS is Masculine: DER BUS
Imagine a boxer jumping on a moving bus.

○ The gender of CAR is Neuter: DAS AUTO
Imagine a car on fire.

○ The gender of TRAIN is Masculine: DER ZUG
Imagine a boxer boarding a train.

YOU CAN WRITE YOUR ANSWERS IN

○ What is the gender and German for train? _____

○ What is the gender and German for car? _____

○ What is the gender and German for bus? _____

○ What is the gender and German for ladies? _____

○ What is the gender and German for gentlemen? _____

○ What is the gender and German for toilet? _____

○ What is the gender and German for customs? _____

○ What is the gender and German for suitcase? _____

○ What is the gender and German for money? _____

○ What is the gender and German for passport? _____

TURN BACK FOR THE ANSWERS

SOME MORE TRAVELLING WORDS

THINK OF EACH IMAGE IN YOUR MIND'S EYE FOR ABOUT TEN SECONDS

○ The German for MAP is KARTE   (KARTEH)
Imagine Ex-President Jimmy CARTER reading a map.

○ The German for STATION is BAHNHOF (BAHNHOHF)
Imagine a BARN with HOOF marks at the
entrance. As you watch, a train comes out
and you see it is a station.

○ The German for GARAGE is GARAGE (GARAHGE)
Imagine a GARAGE with German flag flying from it.

○ The German for EXHAUST is AUSPUFF (OWSPUF)
Imagine PUFFING OUT dirty black smoke from your
exhaust.

○ The German for PUNCTURE is PANNE (PANNEH)
Imagine running over a PAN in the road
which causes a puncture.

○ The German for WHEEL is RAD   (RAHD)
Imagine a RAT squashed under your car wheel.

○ The German for TYRE is REIFEN   (RIFEN)*
Imagine someone with a RIFLE poking your tyre.

○ The German for CLUTCH is KUPPLUNG (KUPLUNG)
Imagine the COUPLING between the engine
and the gears — the clutch.

○ The German for OIL is ÖL   (E(r)L)
Imagine a tin of OIL standing on the German flag.

○ The German for PETROL is BENZIN (BENTSEEN)
Imagine BENZINE for sale in a petrol station.

* The I is pronounced like the I in "wine".

YOU CAN WRITE YOUR ANSWERS IN

○ What is the English for Benzin? _____

○ What is the English for Öl? _____

○ What is the English for Kupplung? _____

○ What is the English for Reifen? _____

○ What is the English for Rad? _____

○ What is the English for Panne? _____

○ What is the English for Auspuff? _____

○ What is the English for Garage? _____

○ What is the English for Bahnhof? _____

○ What is the English for Karte? _____

TURN BACK FOR THE ANSWERS

GENDERS

THINK OF EACH IMAGE IN YOUR MIND'S EYE FOR ABOUT TEN SECONDS

○ The gender of MAP is Feminine: DIE KARTE
Imagine a little girl trying to follow directions with a map.

○ The gender of STATION is Masculine: DER BAHNHOF
Imagine a boxer buying a ticket at a railway station.

○ The gender of GARAGE is Feminine: DIE GARAGE
Imagine a little girl at a garage.

○ The gender of EXHAUST is Masculine: DER AUSPUFF
Imagine a boxer tying a broken exhaust back on a car.

○ The gender of PUNCTURE is Feminine: DIE PANNE
Imagine a little girl trying to mend a puncture on a car tyre.

○ The gender of WHEEL is Neuter: DAS RAD
Imagine a wheel driving through a fire.

○ The gender of TYRE is Masculine: DER REIFEN
Imagine a boxer with a tyre around his waist.

○ The gender of CLUTCH is Feminine: DIE KUPPLUNG
Imagine a little girl trying to press in the clutch pedal.

○ The gender of OIL is Neuter: DAS ÖL
Imagine throwing thick black oil onto a
fire and causing thick black smoke.

○ The gender of PETROL is Neuter: DAS BENZIN
Imagine throwing petrol on a fire and watching it flare up.

YOU CAN WRITE YOUR ANSWERS IN

○ What is the gender and German for petrol? _____

○ What is the gender and German for oil? _____

○ What is the gender and German for clutch? _____

○ What is the gender and German for tyre? _____

○ What is the gender and German for wheel? _____

○ What is the gender and German for
puncture? _____

○ What is the gender and German for
exhaust? _____

○ What is the gender and German for garage? _____

○ What is the gender and German for station? _____

○ What is the gender and German for map? _____

TURN BACK FOR THE ANSWERS

166

SOME MORE USEFUL WORDS

THINK OF EACH IMAGE IN YOUR MIND'S EYE FOR ABOUT TEN SECONDS

○ The German for MY is MEIN   (MINE)
   Imagine thinking "That is MY MINE. I will explode it."

○ The German for YOUR (to a friend) is DEIN   (DINE)*
   Imagine telling your mother "I will not DINE at YOUR
   table."

○ The German for HIS is SEIN   (ZINE)*
   Imagine being told by someone to wait for
   HIS SIGN, before morning.
   (SEIN is also the German for ITS)

○ The German for HER is IHR   (EER)
   Imagine having to whisper in HER EAR.
   (IHR is also the German for THEIR and YOUR
   when you are not familiar with the person)

○ The German for OUR is UNSER   (UNSER)*
   Imagine wishing that OUR house was in WINDSOR.

○ The German for YOUR (formal) is IHR   (EER)
   Imagine telling a group of people: "Put your hands
   on YOUR EARS."

* The I is pronounced like the I in "wine", the U like the U in "put".

YOU CAN WRITE YOUR ANSWERS IN

○ What is the English for Ihr? _____

○ What is the English for unser? _____

○ What is the English for ihr? _____

○ What is the English for sein? _____

○ What is the English for dein? _____

○ What is the English for mein? _____

TURN BACK FOR THE ANSWERS

YOU CAN WRITE YOUR ANSWERS IN

○ **What is the German for your?** _____

○ **What is the German for our?** _____

○ **What is the German for her?** _____

○ **What is the German for his?** _____

○ **What is the German for your?** _____

○ **What is the German for my?** _____

TURN BACK FOR THE ANSWERS

ELEMENTARY GRAMMAR

To use the words MEIN, DEIN, and so on, you change the end of the word exactly as you do for the word EIN.

In the MASCULINE you say,

EIN VATER IST GROSS   (A father is big)
MEIN VATER IST GROSS (My father is big)
DEIN VATER IST GROSS (Your father is big)

Similarly,

IT LOVES A FATHER   is ES LIEBT EIN*EN* VATER
IT LOVES MY FATHER is ES LIEBT MEIN*EN* VATER

In the FEMININE:

A DUCK IS BIG   is EINE ENTE IST GROSS
MY DUCK IS BIG   is MEINE ENTE IST GROSS
IT LOVES A DUCK   is ES LIEBT EIN*E* ENTE
IT LOVES MY DUCK is ES LIEBT MEIN*E* ENTE

In the NEUTER:

A PIG IS BIG   is *EIN* SCHWEIN IST GROSS
MY PIG IS BIG   is *MEIN* SCHWEIN IST GROSS
IT LOVES A PIG   is ES LIEBT *EIN* SCHWEIN
IT LOVES YOUR PIG is ES LIEBT *DEIN* SCHWEIN

Now translate the following:

(You can write your answers in)

1. MY MONEY IS HERE
2. YOUR SISTER IS NOT VERY WHITE
3. YOUR COW HAS A SUITCASE (not to a friend)
4. HIS TOILET IS EMPTY
5. IT HAS YOUR CAR

The answers are:

1. MEIN GELD IST HIER
2. DEINE SCHWESTER IST NICHT SEHR WEISS
3. IHRE KUH HAT EINEN HANDKOFFER
4. SEINE TOILETTE IST LEER
5. ES HAT DEIN AUTO

Now cover up the answers below and translate the following:

(You can write your answers in)

1. MEIN VATER LIEBT SEIN AUTO, ABER MEINE
   MUTTER LIEBT IHR PFERD

2. MEIN REISEPASS IST SEHR NETT, ABER DEINE
   TOILETTE IST SEHR SCHLECHT

3. DAS RAD UND DER AUSPUFF SIND BILLIG, ABER
   DEINE KUPPLUNG UND DEIN REIFEN SIND TEUER

4. ER HAT ZWEI PANNEN, UND DER ZUG IST SPÄT

5. UNSER BUS IST SPÄT

The answers are:

1. MY FATHER LOVES HIS CAR, BUT MY MOTHER LOVES
   HER HORSE

2. MY PASSPORT IS VERY NICE, BUT YOUR TOILET IS
   VERY BAD

3. THE WHEEL AND THE EXHAUST ARE CHEAP, BUT
   YOUR CLUTCH AND YOUR TYRE ARE EXPENSIVE

4. HE HAS TWO PUNCTURES AND THE TRAIN IS LATE

5. OUR BUS IS LATE

Now cover up the answers below and translate the following:

(You can write your answers in)

1. MEINE FORELLE HAT ZWEI REIFEN, FÜNF TOMATEN UND EINE WURST

2. WARUM IST DER ZUG SPÄT?

3. MEIN BRUDER IST SEHR GROSS, ABER MEINE SCHWESTER IST SEHR KLEIN

4. DER JUNGE LIEBT SEINEN SCHECK, UND DU LIEBST DEINEN VATER

5. DAS MÄDCHEN UND DER JUNGE ESSEN ZWEI EIER, UND ICH ESSE SIEBEN BIRNEN

The answers are:

1. MY TROUT HAS TWO TYRES, FIVE TOMATOES AND A SAUSAGE

2. WHY IS THE TRAIN LATE?

3. MY BROTHER IS VERY BIG, BUT MY SISTER IS VERY SMALL

4. THE BOY LOVES HIS CHEQUE, AND YOU LOVE YOUR FATHER

5. THE GIRL AND THE BOY EAT TWO EGGS, AND I EAT SEVEN PEARS

(Note: The plural of EI is EIER).

Do not worry if you did not get many right. No-one gets them all correct at the first attempt. Even if you make a mistake with the endings you will be understood.

The important thing at this stage is to know why endings are sometimes different.

You can go on to the next section even if you are making mistakes at this stage.

Section 9 LEISURE ACTIVITY

ON THE BEACH AND LEISURE

THINK OF EACH IMAGE IN YOUR MIND'S EYE FOR ABOUT TEN SECONDS

○ The German for BEACH is STRAND   (SHTRANT)
Imagine being STRANDED on a beach.

○ The German for HEAT is HITZE   (HITSEH)
Imagine someone so demented by the heat that
he goes up to a woman and HITS HER.

○ The German for COLD is KÄLTE   (KELTEH)
Imagine that it is so cold that it KILLED HER.

○ The German for RIVER is FLUSS   (FLUSS)*
Imagine candy-FLOSS floating on a river.

○ The German for FOREST is WALD   (VALT)
Imagine running WILD through a forest.

○ The German for MOUNTAIN is BERG   (BERG)
Imagine an iceBERG on top of a mountain.

○ The German for CAMERA is KAMERA   (KAMERA)
Imagine a CAMERA placed on a German flag.

○ The German for LETTER is BRIEF   (BREEF)
Imagine writing a BRIEF letter.

○ The German for NEWSPAPER is ZEITUNG   (TSITUNG)*
Imagine you SIGH "TONGUE" as you see
your favourite cold tongue salad spilled all over the newspaper.

○ The German for BOOK is BUCH   (BOOCH)
Imagine a BOOK lying on the German flag.

* The I is pronounced like the I in "wine", the U like the U in "put".

YOU CAN WRITE YOUR ANSWERS IN

○ What is the English for Buch? _____

○ What is the English for Zeitung? _____

○ What is the English for Brief? _____

○ What is the English for Kamera? _____

○ What is the English for Berg? _____

○ What is the English for Wald? _____

○ What is the English for Fluss? _____

○ What is the English for Kälte? _____

○ What is the English for Hitze? _____

○ What is the English for Strand? _____

TURN BACK FOR THE ANSWERS

GENDERS

THINK OF EACH IMAGE IN YOUR MIND'S EYE FOR ABOUT TEN SECONDS

○ The gender of BEACH is Masculine: DER STRAND
Imagine two boxers fighting on the beach.

○ The gender of HEAT is Feminine: DIE HITZE
Imagine a little girl collapsing as the heat hits her.

○ The gender of COLD is Feminine: DIE KÄLTE
Imagine a little girl freezing in the cold.

○ The gender of RIVER is Masculine: DER FLUSS
Imagine a boxer swimming in a river with his boxing gloves on.

○ The gender of FOREST is Masculine: DER WALD
Imagine a boxer training by running through a forest.

○ The gender of MOUNTAIN is Masculine: DER BERG
Imagine a boxing match on the top of a mountain.

○ The gender of CAMERA is Feminine: DIE KAMERA
Imagine a little girl taking photographs with a camera.

○ The gender of LETTER is Masculine: DER BRIEF
Imagine a boxer stuffing a letter down his briefs.

○ The gender of NEWSPAPER is Feminine: DIE ZEITUNG
Imagine a little girl reading a newspaper.

○ The gender of BOOK is Neuter: DAS BUCH
Imagine throwing a book onto a fire and watching it burn.

YOU CAN WRITE YOUR ANSWERS IN

○ What is the gender and German for Book? _____

○ What is the gender and German for
Newspaper? _____

○ What is the gender and German for Letter? _____

○ What is the gender and German for
Camera? _____

○ What is the gender and German for
Mountain? _____

○ What is the gender and German for Forest? _____

○ What is the gender and German for River? _____

○ What is the gender and German for Cold? _____

○ What is the gender and German for Heat? _____

○ What is the gender and German for Beach? _____

TURN BACK FOR THE ANSWERS

SOME USEFUL WORDS

THINK OF EACH IMAGE IN YOUR MIND'S EYE FOR ABOUT TEN SECONDS

○ The German for DOCTOR is ARZT   (ARTST)
Imagine a doctor operating in the middle of
the room with works of ART all around him.

○ The German for DENTIST is ZAHNARZT (TSAHNARTST)
Imagine a dentist drilling a hole in a work of ZEN ART.

○ The German for POLICE is POLIZEI   (POLITSI)*
Imagine a German POLICEMAN holding a German flag.

○ The German for CHEMIST'S SHOP is APOTHEKE
Imagine the old chemist sign   (APOTAIKEH)
'APOTHECARY' above a chemist's shop.

○ The German for HAIR DRESSER is FRISEUR (FREESUR)
Imagine your hair dresser FRIZZING your hair.

○ The German for POST OFFICE is POST   (POST)
Imagine a POST office with a German flag flying outside.

○ The German for BANK is BANK   (BANK)
Imagine your local BANK draped in German flag.

○ The German for HOTEL is HOTEL   (HOTEL)
Imagine German flags all round the HOTEL where you stay.

○ The German for MUSEUM is MUSEUM   (MOOSAIUM)
Imagine the Imperial War MUSEUM with
an exhibition of German flags.

○ The German for CATHEDRAL is DOM   (DOHM)
Imagine looking at the huge DOME of a cathedral.

* The second I is pronounced like the I in "wine".

YOU CAN WRITE YOUR ANSWERS IN

○ What is the English for Dom? _____

○ What is the English for Museum? _____

○ What is the English for Hotel? _____

○ What is the English for Bank? _____

○ What is the English for Post? _____

○ What is the English for Friseur? _____

○ What is the English for Apotheke? _____

○ What is the English for Polizei? _____

○ What is the English for Zahnarzt? _____

○ What is the English for Arzt? _____

TURN BACK FOR THE ANSWERS

GENDERS

THINK OF EACH IMAGE IN YOUR MIND'S EYE FOR ABOUT TEN SECONDS

○ The gender of DOCTOR is Masculine: DER ARZT
Imagine a doctor examining a boxer who has been knocked out.

○ The gender of DENTIST is Masculine: DER ZAHNARZT
Imagine a dentist trying to put a boxer's teeth back in.

○ The gender of POLICE is Feminine: DIE POLIZEI
Imagine a little girl talking to the police.

○ The gender of CHEMIST'S SHOP is Feminine:
DIE APOTHEKE
Imagine a little girl going round to the chemist to buy aspirin for her headache.

○ The gender of HAIR DRESSER is Masculine:
DER ERISEUR
Imagine a hair dresser giving a boxer a very short haircut.

○ The gender of POST OFFICE is Feminine: DIE POST
Imagine a little girl going to the local post office to buy a stamp.

○ The gender of BANK is Feminine: DIE BANK
Imagine a little girl trying to reach up to a bank counter to put money into her account.

○ The gender of HOTEL is Neuter: DAS HOTEL
Imagine a fire sweeping through an hotel, with guests jumping out of upper storey windows.

○ The gender of MUSEUM is Neuter: DAS MUSEUM
Imagine a fire in a big museum, destroying the priceless Egyptian mummies and vases.

○ The gender of CATHEDRAL is Masculine: DER DOM
Imagine a boxing match inside Westminster Cathedral.

YOU CAN WRITE YOUR ANSWERS IN

○ What is the gender and German for cathedral? _____

○ What is the gender and German for museum? _____

○ What is the gender and German for hotel? _____

○ What is the gender and German for bank? _____

○ What is the gender and German for post office? _____

○ What is the gender and German for hair dresser? _____

○ What is the gender and German for chemist's shop? _____

○ What is the gender and German for police? _____

○ What is the gender and German for dentist? _____

○ What is the gender and German for doctor? _____

TURN BACK FOR THE ANSWERS

SOME MORE USEFUL WORDS

THINK OF EACH IMAGE IN YOUR MIND'S EYE FOR ABOUT TEN SECONDS

○ The German for WITH is MIT   (MIT)
Imagine your hand WITH a MITTEN on.

○ The German for WITHOUT is OHNE   (OHNEH)
Imagine an OWNER WITHOUT what he owns.

○ The German for THROUGH is DURCH   (DURCH)*
Imagine going THROUGH DOORs.

○ The German for AGAINST is GEGEN   (GAIGEN)
Imagine someone holding a GAY GUN AGAINST your head.

○ The German for ON is AUF   (OWF)
Imagine someone going "OWF" when you hit him ON the head.

○ The German for FOR is FÜR   (FOOR)
Imagine being FOR FUR and against plastic.

○ The German for ABOVE is ÜBER   (OOBER)
Imagine a HOOVER ABOVE your head.

○ The German for UNDER is UNTER   (UNTER)*
Imagine crawling UNDER the German flag.

○ The German for BESIDE is NEBEN   (NAIBEN)
Imagine thinking "There's NO BIN BESIDE me."

○ The German for IN is IN   (IN)
Imagine being IN an INN.

* The U is pronounced like the U in "put".

YOU CAN WRITE YOUR ANSWERS IN

○ **What is the English for in?** _____

○ **What is the English for neben?** _____

○ **What is the English for unter?** _____

○ **What is the English for über?** _____

○ **What is the English for für?** _____

○ **What is the English for auf?** _____

○ **What is the English for gegen?** _____

○ **What is the English for durch?** _____

○ **What is the English for ohne?** _____

○ **What is the English for mit?** _____

TURN BACK FOR THE ANSWERS

YOU CAN WRITE YOUR ANSWERS IN

○ What is the German for in? _____

○ What is the German for beside? _____

○ What is the German for under? _____

○ What is the German for above? _____

○ What is the German for for? _____

○ What is the German for on? _____

○ What is the German for against? _____

○ What is the German for through? _____

○ What is the German for without? _____

○ What is the German for with? _____

TURN BACK FOR THE ANSWERS

ELEMENTARY GRAMMAR

When you use the words ON, IN, UNDER, OVER, etc., then these words indicate the place of an object.

For example,

A DOG IS ON THE TABLE

A DOG IS UNDER THE TABLE

A DOG IS OVER THE TABLE

When this happens, the word THE after on, under, etc., is often DEM.

For example,

A DOG IS ON THE TABLE is EIN HUND IST AUF *DEM* TISCH

A DOG IS UNDER THE TABLE is EIN HUND IST UNTER *DEM* TISCH

(Imagine a dog on A DAMNED table)

The same is true for NEUTER words:

ON THE PIG is AUF *DEM* SCHWEIN

UNDER THE PIG is UNTER *DEM* SCHWEIN

For FEMININE words, curiously, the word THE is DER in this case:

UNDER THE CAT is UNTER *DER* KATZE

OVER THE CAT is ÜBER *DER* KATZE

Words like MEIN, DEIN and so on take the same ending as the word THE.

So,

MASCULINE

ON MY DOG is AUF MEINEM HUND

FEMININE

ON MY CAT is AUF MEINER KATZE

NEUTER

ON MY PIG is AUF MEINEM SCHWEIN

Now cover up the answers below and translate the following:

(You can write your answers in)

1. THE SPIDER IS ON THE LETTER
2. THE DOG AND THE CAT ARE UNDER THE NEWSPAPER
3. THE PIANO IS ON MY MOTHER
4. THE MONEY IS WITH MY BROTHER
5. THE MONEY IS UNDER THE HORSE

The answers are:

1. DIE SPINNE IST AUF DEM BRIEF
2. DER HUND UND DIE KATZE SIND UNTER DER ZEITUNG
3. DAS KLAVIER IST AUF MEINER MUTTER
4. DAS GELD IST MIT MEINEM BRUDER
5. DAS GELD IST UNTER DEM PFERD

Now cover up the answers below and translate the following:

(You can write your answers in)

1. DAS BUCH IST IN DEM WALD

2. DAS MUSEUM UND DAS HOTEL SIND AUF DEM BERG

3. DIE BANK IST OHNE GELD, UND DER FRISEUR IST SEHR TEUER

4. DER ARZT UND DER ZAHNARZT SIND IN EINEM BERUF

5. DIE POLIZEI IST MIT MEINER MUTTER UND MIT MEINEM VATER

The answers are:

1. THE BOOK IS IN THE FOREST

2. THE MUSUEM AND THE HOTEL ARE ON THE MOUNTAIN

3. THE BANK IS WITHOUT MONEY, AND THE HAIR-DRESSER IS VERY EXPENSIVE

4. THE DOCTOR AND THE DENTIST ARE IN A PROFESSION

5. THE POLICE ARE WITH MY MOTHER AND WITH MY FATHER

ELEMENTARY GRAMMAR

A big confusion arises for masculine words coming after words like IN or ON etc.

You use DEM e.g. Auf DEM Tisch when the verb before is not active as in, The dog IS on the table.

Where the verb before is active e.g. The dog GOES on the table, you use DEN just as you normally do, Auf DEN Tisch.

For neuter words you also use DEM after an inactive verb e.g. The dog IS on the pig is . . . auf DEM Schwein, and you use DAS after an active verb. So, The dog GOES on the pig is . . . auf DAS Schwein.

For feminine words you use DER following the inactive verb and DIE following the active verb. So, . . . IS on the cow is . . . auf DER Kuh and GOES on the cow is . . . auf DIE Kuh.

Do not worry about making mistakes as long as you understand why there are differences between DEM, DEN, etc.

Now cover up the answers below and translate the following:

(You can write your answers in)

1. THE BOY GOES IN THE RIVER
2. THE GIRL IS IN THE RIVER
3. THE HORSE GOES OVER THE BOOK
4. THE HORSE IS ON THE LAWN
5. THE LETTER IS ON THE COW

The answers are:

1. DER JUNGE GEHT IN DEN FLUSS
2. DAS MÄDCHEN IST IN DEM FLUSS
3. DAS PFERD GEHT ÜBER DAS BUCH
4. DAS PFERD IST AUF DEM RASEN
5. DER BRIEF IST AUF DER KUH

Now cover up the answers below and translate the following:

(You can write your answers in)

1. DAS MÄDCHEN GEHT DURCH DEN ZOLL
2. DAS ÖL UND DAS BENZIN SIND IN DEM AUTO IN DER GARAGE
3. DIE HITZE GEHT DURCH DIE APOTHEKE
4. DIE KAMERA IST AUF DEM BETT
5. DIE POST UND DER DOM SIND AUF DEM RASEN
6. ER WAR FÜNF MINUTEN IN DEM RESTAURANT

The answers are:

1. THE GIRL GOES THROUGH THE CUSTOMS
2. THE OIL AND THE PETROL ARE IN THE CAR IN THE GARAGE
3. THE HEAT GOES THROUGH THE CHEMIST'S SHOP
4. THE CAMERA IS ON THE BED
5. THE POST OFFICE AND THE CATHEDRAL ARE ON THE LAWN
6. HE WAS FIVE MINUTES IN THE RESTAURANT

DAYS OF THE WEEK

THINK OF EACH IMAGE IN YOUR MIND'S EYE FOR ABOUT TEN SECONDS

The next part deals with days of the week. All but one of the days of the week end with the word TAG — the German word for day.

The images you will be given will therefore concentrate on the first part of the word.

○ The German for MONDAY is MONTAG   (MOHNTAHG)
Imagine MOANING because Monday is
here and you have to go to work.

○ The German for TUESDAY is DIENSTAG   (DEENSTAHG)
Imagine Tuesday is when the DEANS of
the University faculties always meet.

○ The German for WEDNESDAY is MITTWOCH (MITVOCH)
Imagine that Wednesday is MIDWEEK.

○ The German for THURSDAY is DONNERSTAG
Imagine every Thursday at DAWN you   (DONNERSTAHG)
watch a stag drinking — at DAWN A STAG on Thursday.

○ The German for FRIDAY is FREITAG   (FRITAHG)*
Imagine after the last day of the week you have a FRY UP
for tea because you are tired — Friday is FRY TAG.

○ The German for SATURDAY is SAMSTAG   (ZAMSTAHG)
Imagine a friend called Sam always visits
you on Saturday — SAM'S TAG.

○ The German for SUNDAY is SONNTAG   (ZONNTAHG)
Imagine the SUN shines on Sundays — SUN TAG.

* The I is pronounced like the I in "wine".

Please note that the word ON when used with the day of the week is AM.

So,

ON TUESDAY is AM DIENSTAG

YOU CAN WRITE YOUR ANSWERS IN

○ What is the English for Sonntag? _____

○ What is the English for Samstag? _____

○ What is the English for Freitag? _____

○ What is the English for Donnerstag? _____

○ What is the English for Mittwoch? _____

○ What is the English for Dienstag? _____

○ What is the English for Montag? _____

TURN BACK FOR THE ANSWERS

YOU CAN WRITE YOUR ANSWERS IN

○ **What is the German for Sunday?** _____

○ **What is the German for Saturday?** _____

○ **What is the German for Friday?** _____

○ **What is the German for Thursday?** _____

○ **What is the German for Wednesday?** _____

○ **What is the German for Tuesday?** _____

○ **What is the German for Monday?** _____

TURN BACK FOR THE ANSWERS

Now cover up the answers below and translate the following:

(You can write your answers in)

1. IT IS TUESDAY, AND TOMORROW IS WEDNESDAY
2. ON THURSDAY THE DOG GOES IN THE RIVER
3. ON FRIDAY AND SATURDAY IT WAS COLD
4. ON SUNDAY I AM GOING IN THE FOREST
5. ON MONDAY I WAS VERY TIRED

The answers are:

1. ES IST DIENSTAG, UND MORGEN IST ES MITTWOCH
2. AM DONNERSTAG GEHT DER HUND IN DEN FLUSS
3. AM FREITAG UND SAMSTAG WAR ES KALT
   (N.B. The word for COLD as an adjective is KALT)
4. AM SONNTAG GEHE ICH IN DEN WALD
5. AM MONTAG WAR ICH SEHR MÜDE

Section 10 AT THE DOCTOR'S, EMERGENCY WORDS, USEFUL WORDS

AT THE DOCTOR'S

THINK OF EACH IMAGE IN YOUR MIND'S EYE FOR ABOUT TEN SECONDS

○ The German for ILL is KRANK   (KRANK)
Imagine having a CRANK as your neighbour, always feeling ill.

○ The German for PAIN is SCHMERZ   (SHMERTS)
Imagine seeing someone who SMARTS with a severe pain.

○ The German for BONE is KNOCHEN   (KNOCHEN)
Imagine KNOCKING two bones together.

○ The German for HEART is HERZ   (HERTS)
Imagine a HERTZ Rent-A-Car with a big heart painted on the side.

○ The German for BLADDER is BLASE   (BLAHSEH)
Imagine feeling BLASE when you find out that your bladder has stopped working properly.

○ The German for EYE is AUGE   (OWGEH)
Imagine a horrible OGRE with one eye staring at you.

○ The German for EAR is OHR   (OHR)
Imagine an OAR from a rowing boat sticking out of both ears.

○ The German for NOSE is NASE   (NAHSEH)
Imagine someone with a very NASAL voice when he speaks through his nose.

○ The German for HAND is HAND   (HANT)
Imagine your HAND holding up a German flag.

○ The German for BLOOD is BLUT   (BLOOT)
Imagine BLOOD on the German flag.

YOU CAN WRITE YOUR ANSWERS IN

○ What is the English for Blut? _____

○ What is the English for Hand? _____

○ What is the English for Nase? _____

○ What is the English for Ohr? _____

○ What is the English for Auge? _____

○ What is the English for Blase? _____

○ What is the English for Herz? _____

○ What is the English for Knochen? _____

○ What is the English for Schmerz? _____

○ What is the English for krank? _____

TURN BACK FOR THE ANSWERS

GENDERS

THINK OF EACH IMAGE IN YOUR MIND'S EYE FOR ABOUT TEN SECONDS

○ The gender of PAIN is Masculine: DER SCHMERZ
  Imagine a boxer writhing in pain.

○ The gender of BONE is Masculine: DER KNOCHEN
  Imagine a boxer hitting his opponent with a large bone.

○ The gender of HEART is Neuter: DAS HERZ
  Imagine feeling that your heart is on the fire.

○ The gender of BLADDER is Feminine: DIE BLASE
  Imagine a little girl who can't control her bladder.

○ The gender of EYE is Neuter: DAS AUGE
  Imagine a huge eye staring at you from the middle of a fire.

○ The gender of EAR is Neuter: DAS OHR
  Imagine burning your ear when you go too close to a fire.

○ The gender of NOSE is Feminine: DIE NASE
  Imagine a a little girl giving her nose a huge blow.

○ The gender of HAND is Feminine: DIE HAND
  Imagine giving a little girl a smack with your hand.

○ The gender of BLOOD is Neuter: DAS BLUT
  Imagine pouring blood onto a fire to try to extinguish it.

PLEASE NOTE:

The word ILL does not have a gender.

YOU CAN WRITE YOUR ANSWERS IN

○ What is the gender and German for blood?   _____

○ What is the gender and German for hand?   _____

○ What is the gender and German for nose?   _____

○ What is the gender and German for ear?   _____

○ What is the gender and German for eye?   _____

○ What is the gender and German for
   bladder?   _____

○ What is the gender and German for heart?   _____

○ What is the gender and German for bone?   _____

○ What is the gender and German for pain?   _____

○ What is the German for ill?   _____

TURN BACK FOR THE ANSWERS

EMERGENCY WORDS

THINK OF EACH IMAGE IN YOUR MIND'S EYE FOR ABOUT TEN SECONDS

O The German for FIRE is FEUER   (FOI ER)
Imagine a fire in the FOYER of a cinema.

O The German for THIEF is DIEB   (DEEP)
Imagine catching a thief and holding
him in a bath of DEEP water.

O The German for AMBULANCE is KRANKENWAGEN
Imagine trying to CRANK up an old   (KRANKENVAHGEN)
WAGON which has a red cross on
the side and was an old ambulance.

O The German for TELEPHONE is TELEFON   (TELEFOHN)
Imagine a TELEPHONE placed on the German flag.

O The German for RAIN is REGEN   (RAIGEN)
Imagine Ronald REAGAN standing in the rain getting wet.

O The German for FOG is NEBEL   (NAIBEL)
Imagine looking for your NAVEL
(belly button) on a very foggy night.

O The German for DOOR is TÜR   (TOOR)
Imagine making a TOUR of your front door.

O The German for JOURNEY is REISE   (RIZEH)*
Imagine RISING early to go on a journey.

O The German for STAIRS is TREPPE   (TREPPEH)
Imagine TRIPPING over the stairs.

O The German for DEATH is TOD   (TOHT)
Imagine finding a dead TOAD.

* The I is pronounced like the I in "wine".

YOU CAN WRITE YOUR ANSWERS IN

○ What is the English for Tod? _____

○ What is the English for Treppe? _____

○ What is the English for Reise? _____

○ What is the English for Tür? _____

○ What is the English for Nebel? _____

○ What is the English for Regen? _____

○ What is the English for Telefon? _____

○ What is the English for Krankenwagen? _____

○ What is the English for Dieb? _____

○ What is the English for Feuer? _____

TURN BACK FOR THE ANSWERS

GENDERS

THINK OF EACH IMAGE IN YOUR MIND'S EYE FOR ABOUT TEN SECONDS

○ The gender of FIRE is Neuter: DAS FEUER
Imagine a fire, it is the symbol of a neuter word in this course.

○ The gender of THIEF is Masculine: DER DIEB
Imagine a thief robbing a boxer whilst he is in the ring fighting.

○ The gender of AMBULANCE is Masculine:
DER KRANKENWAGEN
Imagine taking a boxer to hospital in an ambulance after a fight.

○ The gender of TELEPHONE is Neuter: DAS TELEFON
Imagine throwing a telephone into a fire.

○ The gender of RAIN is Masculine: DER REGEN
Imagine a boxer getting soaking wet from rain in an outdoors fight.

○ The gender of FOG is Masculine: DER NEBEL
Imagine two boxers who miss finding each other in the fog.

○ The gender of DOOR is Feminine: DIE TÜR
Imagine a little girl reaching up to try to open a door.

○ The gender of JOURNEY is Feminine: DIE REISE
Imagine a little girl becoming very excited as she sets out on a long journey.

○ The gender of STAIRS is Feminine: DIE TREPPE
Imagine a little girl tripping down some stairs.
(N.B. Stairs is also a plural noun.)

○ The gender of DEATH is Masculine: DER TOD
Imagine a boxer going to his death.
(The word for DEAD is TOT.)

YOU CAN WRITE YOUR ANSWERS IN

○ **What is the gender and German for death?** _____

○ **What is the gender and German for stairs?** _____

○ **What is the gender and German for journey?** _____

○ **What is the gender and German for door?** _____

○ **What is the gender and German for fog?** _____

○ **What is the gender and German for rain?** _____

○ **What is the gender and German for telephone?** _____

○ **What is the gender and German for ambulance?** _____

○ **What is the gender and German for thief?** _____

○ **What is the gender and German for fire?** _____

TURN BACK FOR THE ANSWERS

SOME MORE USEFUL WORDS

THINK OF EACH IMAGE IN YOUR MIND'S EYE FOR ABOUT TEN SECONDS

○ The German for CAUTION is ACHTUNG   (ACHTUNG)
Imagine being told that you should be
ACTING CAUTIOUSLY.

○ The German for DANGEROUS is GEFÄHRLICH
Imagine you GO A FAIR LICK in your   (GEFAIRLICH)
car, and your passenger shouts "This is DANGEROUS."

○ The German for BE CAREFUL is VORSICHT
Imagine someone shouting "BE   (FOHRSEECHT)
CAREFUL, have FORESIGHT!"

○ The German for LEFT is LINKS   (LINKS)
Imagine driving past LINKS of a chain on
your LEFT hand side as you turn to your left.

○ The German for RIGHT is RECHTS   (RECHTS)
Imagine seeing a whole lot of WRECKED
cars on your RIGHT, as you turn to your right.

○ The German for VACANT is FREI   (FRI)*
Imagine trying to FRY an egg outside a VACANT toilet.

○ The German for ENGAGED is BESETZT   (BESETST)
Imagine someone who has POSSESSED a
toilet and has put the ENGAGED sign on.

○ The German for WRONG is FALSCH   (FALSH)
Imagine accusing someone of being FALSE and WRONG.

○ The German for WET is NASS   (NASS)
Imagine it being WET and NASTY.

○ The German for DRY is TROCKEN   (TROCKEN)
Imagine TRUCKING home on a DRY day.

* The I is pronounced like the I in "wine".

YOU CAN WRITE YOUR ANSWERS IN

○ What is the English for trocken? _____

○ What is the English for nass? _____

○ What is the English for falsch? _____

○ What is the English for besetzt? _____

○ What is the English for frei? _____

○ What is the English for rechts? _____

○ What is the English for links? _____

○ What is the English for Vorsicht? _____

○ What is the English for gefährlich? _____

○ What is the English for Achtung? _____

TURN BACK FOR THE ANSWERS

YOU CAN WRITE YOUR ANSWERS IN

○ What is the German for dry? _____

○ What is the German for wet? _____

○ What is the German for wrong? _____

○ What is the German for engaged? _____

○ What is the German for vacant? _____

○ What is the German for right? _____

○ What is the German for left? _____

○ What is the German for be careful? _____

○ What is the German for dangerous? _____

○ What is the German for caution? _____

TURN BACK FOR THE ANSWERS

Now cover up the answers below and translate the following:

(You can write your answers in)

1. THE PAIN IS IN MY BLADDER
2. I AM ILL
3. THE RAIN IS VERY WET, AND THE FOG IS VERY COLD
4. CAUTION! THE JOURNEY IS ALWAYS DANGEROUS, AND THE CATS ARE BAD
5. THE TELEPHONE IS IN THE AMBULANCE WITH THE THIEF

The answers are:

1. DER SCHMERZ IST IN MEINER BLASE
2. ICH BIN KRANK
3. DER REGEN IST SEHR NASS, UND DER NEBEL IST SEHR KALT

   (KALT is Cold; DIE KÄLTE is The cold).
4. ACHTUNG! DIE REISE IST IMMER GEFÄHRLICH, UND DIE KATZEN SIND SCHLECHT
5. DAS TELEFON IST IN DEM KRANKENWAGEN MIT DEM DIEB

Now cover up the answers below and translate the following:

(You can write your answers in)

1. DAS IST LINKS, UND DAS IST RECHTS

2. ER MACHT DAS FEUER SEHR GROSS

3. ER HAT EINE KLEINE NASE, UND SIE HAT EIN OHR UND EIN HERZ

4. DIE KNOCHEN SIND NASS, ABER DIE AUGEN SIND TROCKEN

5. DIE TOILETTE IST FREI ABER GEFÄHRLICH

The answers are:

1. THAT IS LEFT, AND THAT IS RIGHT

2. HE MAKES THE FIRE VERY BIG

3. HE HAS A SMALL NOSE, AND SHE HAS AN EAR AND A HEART

4. THE BONES ARE WET, BUT THE EYES ARE DRY

5. THE TOILET IS VACANT BUT DANGEROUS

ELEMENTARY GRAMMAR

This final section on grammar will deal with adjective endings.

It is very important that at the start you do not have to worry about endings. They are given at this stage so that you will understand why adjective endings are different in different sentences. Whilst they are a bit complicated, they do follow strict rules, so they can be learnt easily.

When you have the definite article "the" before an adjective like:

THE WHITE DOG IS GREEN

THE BLACK CAT IS GREEN

THE GREEN PIG IS GREEN

then the adjective always ends with an "e".

So,

THE WHITE DOG IS GREEN is DER WEISSE HUND IST GRÜN

THE BLACK CAT IS GREEN is DIE SCHWARZE KATZE IST GRÜN

THE GREEN PIG IS GREEN is DAS GRÜNE SCHWEIN IST GRÜN

When the noun is the object of the sentence — for example:

IT LOVES THE BLACK DOG

IT LOVES THE WHITE CAT

IT LOVES THE GREEN PIG

then for the MASCULINE and FEMININE, the adjective has the same ending as the word "the".

For example,

ES LIEBT DEN SCHWARZEN HUND

ES LIEBT DIE WEISSE KATZE

But for NEUTER the adjective only has the ending "e":

ES LIEBT DAS GRÜNE SCHWEIN

The rule is, therefore, that with the word THE, when the noun is the subject or object of the sentence, an adjective will always end in "E", except when there is a masculine noun as the object of the sentence, when it ends in "EN".

Now cover up the answers below and translate the following:

(You can write your answers in)

1. THE BIG NOSE IS RED
2. THE EMPTY HEART WAS BLACK
3. THE BIG PAIN IS BAD
4. SHE LOVES THE SMALL BLADDER
5. I LOVE THE RED BLOOD

The answers are:

1. DIE GROSSE NASE IST ROT
2. DAS LEERE HERZ WAR SCHWARZ
3. DER GROSSE SCHMERZ IST SCHLECHT
4. SIE LIEBT DIE KLEINE BLASE
5. ICH LIEBE DAS ROTE BLUT

Now cover up the answers below and translate the following:

(You can write your answers in)

1. DIE WEISSE HAND WAR KALT
2. DAS GROSSE OHR IST GRÜN
3. ICH ESSE DAS SCHWERE HERZ
4. ER LIEBT DAS SCHWARZE AUGE
5. SIE LIEBEN DIE KLEINE NASE

The answers are:

1. THE WHITE HAND WAS COLD
2. THE BIG EAR IS GREEN
3. I EAT THE HEAVY HEART
4. HE LOVES THE BLACK EYE
5. YOU (or THEY) LOVE THE LITTLE NOSE

ELEMENTARY GRAMMAR

When you use the word "a", as in:

A WHITE DOG IS GREEN
A BLACK CAT IS GREEN
A GREEN PIG IS GREEN

then the adjective ending is the same as the ending of the word THE.

So,

A WHITE DOG IS GREEN is	EIN WEISS*ER* HUND IST GRÜN
A BLACK CAT IS GREEN is	EINE SCWARZ*E* KATZE IST GRÜN
A GREEN PIG IS GREEN is	EIN GRÜN*ES* SCHWEIN IST GRÜN

When the noun is the object of the sentence:

IT LOVES A WHITE DOG
IT LOVES A BLACK CAT
IT LOVES A GREEN PIG

then again the adjectives takes the same ending as the definite article THE:

IT LOVES A WHITE DOG is	ES LIEBT EINEN WEISS*EN* HUND
IT LOVES A BLACK CAT is	ES LIEBT EINE SCHWARZ*E* KATZE
IT LOVES A GREEN PIG is	ES LIEBT EIN GRÜN*ES* SCHWEIN

DO NOT WORRY ABOUT THE ADJECTIVE ENDINGS TO BEGIN WITH.

Provided you understand what has been written above, you will be able to understand spoken German.

As you use German, you will come to use the adjective endings correctly, and it would be a great pity if you stopped to think too much about adjective endings before you spoke. The odd mistake to begin with will not stop you being understood when you speak.

PLEASE NOTE that the words MEIN, DEIN, SEIN, IHR, UNSER all end in the same way as EIN.

So,

A WHITE DOG IS GREEN is	EIN WEISS*ER* HUND IST GRÜN
MY WHITE DOG IS GREEN is	MEIN WEISS*ER* HUND IST GRÜN
YOUR WHITE DOG IS GREEN is	DEIN WEISS*ER* HUND IST GRÜN

and so on.

Now cover up the answers below and translate the following:

(You can write your answers in)

1. THE BIG DUCK WAS DEAD, BUT THE WHITE HORSE IS NOT DEAD

2. IT IS A WET RAIN AND A DRY FOG

3. MY BIG BANK HAS MUCH (a lot of) MONEY

4. WHY IS IT ENGAGED?

5. THE WIFE LOVES A LITTLE DOOR

The answers are:

1. DIE GROSSE ENTE WAR TOT, ABER DAS WEISSE PFERD IST NICHT TOT

2. ES IST EIN NASSER REGEN UND EIN TROCKENER NEBEL

3. MEINE GROSSE BANK HAT VIEL GELD

4. WARUM IST ES BESETZT?

5. DIE FRAU LIEBT EINE KLEINE TÜR

Please do not worry if you did not get the adjective endings right. You will always be understood even if you got the endings wrong.

Now cover up the answers below and translate the following:

(You can write your answers in)

1. ICH MACHE EINE WEISSE TÜR
2. ICH ESSE EINE KLEINE TOMATE
3. SIE HABEN EINEN GROSSEN HUND
4. ER MACHT EINE KLEINE KATZE
5. ER IST EIN GROSSER SOHN

The answers are:

1. I AM MAKING A WHITE DOOR
2. I AM EATING A SMALL TOMATO
3. YOU (or THEY) HAVE A BIG DOG
4. HE IS MAKING A SMALL CAT
5. HE IS A BIG SON

THE MONTHS OF THE YEAR
As the months of the year sound very similar to their English counterparts, images will not be given.

English	German	Pronounced
January	JANUAR	YANOO AR
February	FEBRUAR	FEBROO AR
March	MÄRZ	MERTS
April	APRIL	APREEL
May	MAI	MI*
June	JUNI	YOONEE
July	JULI	YOOLEE
August	AUGUST	OWGUST
September	SEPTEMBER	ZEPTEMBER
October	OKTOBER	OKTOHBER
November	NOVEMBER	NOVEMBER
December	DEZEMBER	DEHTSEMBER

* The I is pronounced like the I in "wine".

When you say IN DECEMBER or IN JANUARY, etc., then the word for IN is IM.

So,

IN DECEMBER is IM DEZEMBER

IN MARCH is IM MÄRZ

YOU CAN WRITE YOUR ANSWERS IN

O **What is the English for Januar?** _____

O **What is the English for Februar?** _____

O **What is the English for März?** _____

O **What is the English for April?** _____

O **What is the English for Mai?** _____

O **What is the English for Juni?** _____

O **What is the English for Juli?** _____

O **What is the English for August?** _____

O **What is the English for September?** _____

O **What is the English for Oktober?** _____

O **What is the English for November?** _____

O **What is the English for Dezember?** _____

TURN BACK FOR THE ANSWERS

YOU CAN WRITE YOUR ANSWERS IN

O **What is the German for January?** _____

O **What is the German for February?** _____

O **What is the German for March?** _____

O **What is the German for April?** _____

O **What is the German for May?** _____

O **What is the German for June?** _____

O **What is the German for July?** _____

O **What is the German for August?** _____

O **What is the German for September?** _____

O **What is the German for October?** _____

O **What is the German for November?** _____

O **What is the German for December?** _____

TURN BACK FOR THE ANSWERS

Now cover up the answers below and translate the following:

(You can write your answers in)

1. IN JANUARY, FEBRUARY AND MARCH IT IS COLD
2. IN APRIL, MAY AND JUNE THE BLOOD IS RED
3. IN JULY AND SEPTEMBER MY MOTHER HAS HOLIDAYS
4. MY FATHER IS HEAVY IN AUGUST AND OCTOBER
5. THE DOCTOR WAS ILL IN NOVEMBER AND DECEMBER

The answers are:

1. IM JANUAR, FEBRUAR UND MÄRZ IST ES KALT
2. IM APRIL, MAI UND JUNI IST DAS BLUT ROT
3. IM JULI UND SEPTEMBER HAT MEINE MUTTER FERIEN
4. MEIN VATER IST SCHWER IM AUGUST UND OKTOBER
5. DER ARZT WAR KRANK IM NOVEMBER UND DEZEMBER

Now cover up the answers below and translate the following:

(You can write your answers in)

1. AM DONNERSTAG MACHE ICH WEIN
2. HEUTE IST ES MITTWOCH
3. ICH WAR MÜDE AM DONNERSTAG
4. AM DIENSTAG GEHE ICH IN DEN FLUSS
5. AM SAMSTAG WAR ES GUT

The answers are:

1. ON THURSDAY I AM MAKING WINE
2. TODAY IT IS WEDNESDAY
3. I WAS TIRED ON THURSDAY
4. ON TUESDAY I AM GOING IN THE RIVER
5. ON SATURDAY IT WAS GOOD

This is the end of the course. We hope you have enjoyed it! Of course words and grammar will not be remembered for ever without revision, but if you look at the book from time to time, you will be surprised at how quickly everything comes back.

When you go abroad, do not be too shy to try out what you have learned. Your host will appreciate your making the effort to speak, even if you are sometimes wrong. And the more you attempt to speak the more you will learn!

GLOSSARY

a	ein/eine	butter	die Butter
above	über	cabbage	der Kohl
after	nach	cake	der Kuchen
against	gegen	camera	die Kamera
also	auch	car	das Auto
always	immer	carpet	der Teppich
am	bin	cash till	die Kasse
ambulance	der Kranken-	cat	die Katze
	wagen	caterpillar	die Raupe
and	und	cathedral	der Dom
apple	der Apfel	caution!	Achtung!
are	bist/sind	cheap	billig
armchair	der Sessel	cheese	der Käse
bacon	der Speck	chemist's	die Apotheke
bad	schlecht	cheque	der Scheck
bank	die Bank	chicken	das Huhn
bathroom	das Badezimmer	clock	die Uhr
be careful!	Vorsicht!	clutch	die Kupplung
beach	der Strand	coat	der Mantel
bean	die Bohne	coffee	der Kaffee
bed	das Bett	cold	die Kälte
bedroom	das Schlaf-	cow	die Kuh
	zimmer	cream	die Sahne
bee	die Biene	cup	die Tasse
before	vor	cupboard	der Schrank
beside	neben	curtain	die Gardine
big	gross	customs	der Zoll
black	schwarz	dangerous	gefährlich
bladder	die Blase	daughter	die Tochter
blood	das Blut	day	der Tag
blouse	die Bluse	dead	tot
blue	blau	dear	teuer
bone	der Knochen	death	der Tod
book	das Buch	deer	der Hirsch
boss	der Chef	dentist	der Zahnarzt
bottle	die Flasche	do	tue
boy	der Junge	doctor	der Arzt
bread	das Brot	does	tut
brother	der Bruder	dog	der Hund
brown	braun	door	die Tür
bull	der Bulle	dress	das Kleid
bus	der Bus	dry	trocken
but	aber	duck	die Ente

ear	das Ohr	holiday	die Ferien
eat	esse	horse	das Pferd
eats	isst	hotel	das Hotel
egg	das Ei	hour	die Stunde
elephant	der Elefant	house	das Haus
empty	leer	how	wie
engaged	besetzt	husband	der Mann
evening	der Abend	I	ich
exhaust	der Auspuff	ill	krank
eye	das Auge	in	in
factory	die Fabrik	is	ist
father	der Vater	jam	die Marmelade
fine	schön	journey	die Reise
fire	das Feuer	kitchen	die Küche
firm	die Firma	knife	das Messer
floor	der Boden	ladies	die Damen
flower	die Blume	late	spät
fog	der Nebel	lawn	der Rasen
for	für	left	links
forest	der Wald	letter	der Brief
fork	die Gabel	light	das Licht
fruit	das Obst	lobster	der Hummer
furniture	die Möbel	loves	liebt
garage	die Garage	make	mache
gentlemen	die Herren	makes	macht
girl	das Mädchen	manager	der Leiter
give	gebe	map	die Karte
gives	gibt	market	der Markt
go	gehe	meat	das Fleisch
goes	geht	menu	die Speisekarte
good	gut	midge	die Mücke
goose	die Gans	milk	die Milch
green	grün	minute	die Minute
grey	grau	mistake	der Fehler
hairdresser	der Friseur	money	das Geld
half	halb	month	der Monat
hand	die Hand	more	mehr
has	hat	morning	der Morgen
hat	der Hut	moth	die Motte
have	habe	mother	die Mutter
he	er	mountain	der Berg
heart	das Herz	mouse	die Maus
heat	die Hitze	much	viel
heavy	schwer	museum	das Museum
her	ihr	mushroom	der Pilz
here	hier	my	mein
his	sein	nasty	eklig

newspaper	die Zeitung	saucer	die Untertasse
nice	nett	sausage	die Wurst
no	nein	second	die Sekunde
noisy	laut	she	sie
nose	die Nase	shelf	das Brett
not	nicht	shirt	das Hemd
of course	natürlich	shoe	der Schuh
office	das Büro	short	kurz
oil	das Öl	sister	die Schwester
on	auf	skirt	der Rock
onion	die Zwiebel	small	klein
only	nur	socks	die Socken
or	oder	son	der Sohn
orange	orange	soon	bald
our	unser	sorry	Entschuldigung!
owner	der Besitzer	soup	die Suppe
pain	der Schmerz	spider	die Spinne
passport	der Reisepass	spoon	der Löffel
pea	die Erbse	stairs	die Treppe
pear	die Birne	station	der Bahnhof
petrol	das Benzin	still	noch
piano	das Klavier	suitcase	der Handkoffer
picture	das Bild	table	der Tisch
pig	das Schwein	take	nehme
plate	der Teller	takes	nimmt
please	bitte	tea	der Tee
police	die Polizei	telephone	das Telefon
post office	die Post	thanks	danke
potato	die Kartoffel	that	das
price	der Preis	the	der/die/das
product	das Produkt	there	da
profession	der Beruf	thief	der Dieb
puncture	die Panne	thing	die Sache
quarter	viertel	this	dies
quick	schnell	through	durch
quite	ganz	tie	der Schlips
rain	der Regen	time	die Zeit
receipt	die Quittung	tired	müde
red	rot	today	heute
restaurant	das Restaurant	toilet	die Toilette
right	rechts	tomato	die Tomate
river	der Fluss	tradesman	der Handwerker
roof	das Dach	train	der Zug
room	das Zimmer	training	die Ausbildung
salad	der Salat	tree	der Baum
salary	das Gehalt		
salmon	der Lachs		

trousers	die Hosen	Wednesday	Mittwoch
trout	die Forelle	Thursday	Donnerstag
tyre	der Reifen	Friday	Freitag
under	unter	Saturday	Samstag
vacant	frei		
vegetable	das Gemüse		
very	sehr	**Months of the Year**	
waiter	der Ober	January	Januar
wall	die Wand	February	Februar
was	war	March	März
wasp	die Wespe	April	April
water	das Wasser	May	Mai
watering can	die Giesskanne	June	Juni
week	die Woche	July	Juli
wet	nass	August	August
what	was		
wheel	das Rad		
where	wo	September	September
white	weiss	October	Oktober
who	wer	November	November
why	warum	December	Dezember
wife	die Frau		
window	das Fenster		
wine	der Wein	**Numbers**	
with	mit	one	eins
without	ohne	two	zwei
worker	der Arbeiter	three	drei
worm	der Wurm	four	vier
wrong	falsch	five	fünf
year	das Jahr	six	sechs
yes	ja	seven	sieben
you	du/Sie	eight	acht
your	dein	nine	neun
your	Ihr	ten	zehn
		eleven	elf
		twelve	zwölf
Days of the Week		twenty	zwanzig
Sunday	Sonntag	twenty-five	fünfundzwanzig
Monday	Montag	quarter	viertel
Tuesday	Dienstag	half	halb

226

LINKWORD
LANGUAGE SYSTEM
by Dr Michael M. Gruneberg

LINKWORD is the language course which teaches you how to remember what you learn as you learn it. LINKWORD is the fastest, the easiest, the most enjoyable way to learn a language and is ideal for holidays, business travel and schoolwork!

FOR DETAILS OF HOW TO ORDER AND MORE INFORMATION ABOUT LINKWORD TURN OVER THIS PAGE

LINKWORD AUDIO TAPES

LINKWORD is the language course which teaches you how to remember what you learn as you learn it.

The **LINKWORD** courses teach you hundreds of useful words and a basic grammar and an audio tape is available as an extra learning aid to accompany this book.

It allows you to hear and to practise the correct pronunciation for all the words used on this course.

The tape is available by mail order using the order form at the back of this book, or you can buy the pack from any good bookshop.

LINKWORD AUDIO TAPES

0 552 13225 X	**FRENCH**	0 552 13226 8	**GERMAN**
0 552 13227 6	**SPANISH**	0 552 13228 4	**ITALIAN**
0 552 13966 1	**PORTUGUESE**	0 552 13955 6	**GREEK**
	0 552 14062 7	**FURTHER FRENCH**	

LINKWORD BOOK AND AUDIO TAPE PACKS

The following **LINKWORD** courses are also available in packs combining the books with the relevant pronunciation cassette tape.
These are available either by mail order, using the form at the back of this book, or you can buy the pack from any good bookshop.

0 552 00500 2	**FRENCH**
0 552 00501 0	**SPANISH**
0 552 00370 0	**GERMAN**

LINKWORD
ON COMPUTER

LINKWORD is the language course which teaches you how to remember what you learn as you learn it.

The **LINKWORD** courses teach you hundreds of useful words and a basic grammar and are now available on computer disc.

First Courses
FRENCH * GERMAN * SPANISH * ITALIAN
JAPANESE * GREEK * RUSSIAN * DUTCH
PORTUGUESE * HEBREW

On IBM PC & COMPATIBLES, APPLE II Series.
* Also available on MACINTOSH, S.T. AMIGA, COMMODORE 64 and ACORN RISC O.S.

GCSE LEVEL FRENCH
An extensive vocabulary and grammar up to GCSE level standard, ideal as a follow-up course to the book or first course programs or as a revision or 'brush-up' course for the rusty!

Available on IBM PC & Compatibles.

For further information please contact:

MINERVA SOFTWARE
MINERVA HOUSE
BARING CRESCENT
EXETER
EX1 1TL
TEL: (0392) 437756

ARTWORX INC.
1844 PENFIELD ROAD
PENFIELD
NEW YORK
USA
TEL: (0101 716) 385 6120

LINKWORD LANGUAGE SYSTEM BOOKS, AUDIO TAPES AND BOOK AND TAPE PACKS AVAILABLE FROM CORGI BOOKS

THE PRICES SHOWN BELOW WERE CORRECT AT THE TIME OF GOING TO PRESS. HOWEVER TRANSWORLD PUBLISHERS RESERVE THE RIGHT TO SHOW NEW RETAIL PRICES ON COVERS WHICH MAY DIFFER FROM THOSE PREVIOUSLY ADVERTISED IN THE TEXT OR ELSEWHERE.

☐ 14246 8	**LINKWORD FRENCH IN A DAY**	£3.99
☐ 13053 2	**LINKWORD LANGUAGE COURSE: FRENCH**	£4.99
☐ 13916 5	**LINKWORD LANGUAGE COURSE: FURTHER FRENCH**	£4.99
☐ 13054 0	**LINKWORD LANGUAGE COURSE: GERMAN**	£5.99
☐ 14247 6	**LINKWORD SPANISH IN A DAY**	£3.99
☐ 13055 9	**LINKWORD LANGUAGE COURSE: SPANISH**	£4.99
☐ 13056 7	**LINKWORD LANGUAGE COURSE: ITALIAN**	£5.99
☐ 13907 6	**LINKWORD LANGUAGE COURSE: GREEK**	£4.99
☐ 13906 8	**LINKWORD LANGUAGE COURSE: PORTUGUESE**	£4.99
☐ 13225 X	**LINKWORD AUDIO TAPE: FRENCH**	£6.95*
☐ 14062 7	**LINKWORD AUDIO TAPE: FURTHER FRENCH**	£6.95*
☐ 13226 8	**LINKWORD AUDIO TAPE: GERMAN**	£6.95*
☐ 13227 6	**LINKWORD AUDIO TAPE: SPANISH**	£6.95*
☐ 13228 4	**LINKWORD AUDIO TAPE: ITALIAN**	£6.95*
☐ 13955 6	**LINKWORD AUDIO TAPE: GREEK**	£6.95*
☐ 13966 1	**LINKWORD AUDIO TAPE: PORTUGUESE**	£6.95*
☐ 00500 2	**LINKWORD BOOK AND TAPE PACK: FRENCH**	£11.99*
☐ 00370 0	**LINKWORD BOOK AND TAPE PACK: GERMAN**	£11.99*
☐ 00501 0	**LINKWORD BOOK AND TAPE PACK: SPANISH**	£11.99*

*Inclusive of VAT

All Corgi/Bantam Books are available at your bookshop or newsagent, or can be ordered from the following address:
Corgi/Bantam Books
Cash Sales Department
P.O. Box 11, Falmouth, Cornwall TR10 9EN
UK and B.F.P.O. customers please send a cheque or postal order (no currency) and allow £1.00 for postage and packing for the first book plus 50p for the second book and 30p for each additional book to a maximum charge of £3.00 (7 books plus).

Overseas customers, including Eire, please allow £2.00 for postage and packing for the first book plus £1.00 for the second book and 50p for each subsequent title ordered.

Name . . . .

Address . . . .

. . . .